Biology and Cognitive Development

COGNITIVE DEVELOPMENT

This series presents the work of an outstanding group of scientists working together at the Medical Research Council's Cognitive Development Unit who, in spite of diverse backgrounds, have evolved a common approach to the fundamental issues of cognitive developmental psychology. This is neither nativist nor empiricist, and focuses on the dynamics of change rather than on stages. Covering a range of topics from early infancy onwards, the series will collectively make up a major, new, coherent position.

Also in this series:

Autism   *Uta Frith*

Language and Thought in Normal and Handicapped
Children   *Richard F. Cromer*

Biology and Cognitive Development:

The Case of Face Recognition

Mark H. Johnson and John Morton

BLACKWELL
Oxford UK & Cambridge USA

First published 1991

Basil Blackwell Ltd
108 Cowley Road, Oxford, OX4 1JF, UK

Basil Blackwell, Inc.
3 Cambridge Center
Cambridge, Massachusetts 02142, USA

Library of Congress Cataloging in Publication Data

Johnson, Mark H.
Biology and cognitive development: the case of face recognition/
by Mark H. Johnson and John Morton.
p. cm.—(Cognitive development)
Includes bibliographical references and index.
ISBN 0–631–15949–5 (alk. paper) — ISBN 0–631–17454–0
(pbk.: alk. paper)
1. Face perception—Physiological aspects. 2. Cognition—
Physiological aspects. 3. Developmental psychobiology.
I. Morton, John, 1933– . II. Title. III. Series: Cognitive
development (Oxford, England)
BF242.J64 1991
153.7'5—dc20
91–14953
CIP

British Library Cataloguing in Publication Data

A CIP catalogue record for this book is available from the British Library.

Typeset in 10½/12½pt Plantin
by Hope Services (Abingdon) Ltd.
Printed in Great Britain by T. J. Press Ltd, Padstow, Cornwall

This book is printed on acid-free paper.

Contents

In recognition of our mothers:
Krystyna (Dobraczynska) Johnson and Mary Morton

Preface

Throughout this book we have struggled to balance two different themes; the general theme of how biological factors can be usefully brought into studies of cognitive development, and the specific theme of the developmental mechanisms that underlie face recognition in the human infant. As our title suggests, we use the latter as a case study of the former. While we hope that the majority of our readers will share our general aims, we appreciate that some others may come to the book with a specific interest in one or the other of our two themes. Those with a specific interest in face recognition may prefer to bypass chapters one and three, while those of the opposite inclination may wish to skip the detailed studies of face recognition discussed in chapter five.

Our colleagues Uta Frith and Annette Karmiloff-Smith both struggled womanfully through early drafts. Their (sometimes harsh) comments were crucial in shaping the final form of the book. We are also very grateful to Johan Bolhuis, Keith Darvill, Gabriel Horn, Jim Johnson, Annette Karmiloff-Smith, Jean Mandler and Guinevere Tufnell for reading later drafts of the book. Their comments often sent us back to the drawing board. We also thank our (sometime) colleagues Mike Anderson, Sue Carey, Alan Leslie, Daphne Maurer and Scania de Schonen whose comments and arguments often became incorporated into our thinking, usually without acknowledgement. Needless to say, we are entirely responsible for the final version.

On the experimental side we have been ably assisted at various points in time by Julie Keenan, Julie Philips, Suzanne Dziurawiec and Jon Bartrip. Jon Bartrip was also instrumental in the preparation of this book. Warwick Smith deserves credit for technical assistance and construction of the moving chair apparatus discussed in chapter five.

Leslie Tucker dealt with countless faxes between Pittsburgh and London.

Despite our originally holding very different opinions and theoretial biases, the authors are proud to announce that, six years on, they are still on speaking terms!

Acknowledgements

The authors and publishers are grateful for permission to reproduce the following material:

Figure 1.1 from Fischer, K. W. and Lazerson, A. (1984) *Human Development*, W. H. Freeman and Co. Figure 1.2 from *Changeux*, J.–P. (1983) *L'homme neuronal* © 1983 by Librairie Artheme Fayard. Used with permission. Figure 2.1 from Diamond, R. and Carey, S. (1986) 'Why faces are and are not special: an effect of expertise', *Journal of Experimental Psychology*, 115, 107–17. © 1986 by the American Psychological Society. Used with permission. Figure 2.2 from Atkinson, J. and Braddick, O. (1983) 'Human visual development'. In Nicholson, J. and Foss, B. (eds) *Psychological Survey No. 4*, British Psychological Society. Used with permission. Figure 2.4 Used by kind permission of the artist, Priscilla Barrett. Figure 3.1 Used by kind permission of H. R. Rodman. Figure 3.2 Reproduced by kind permission of Keith M. Kendrick. Figure 3.3 from Horn, G. (1985) *Memory, Imprinting and the Brain*, Clarendon Press. Reproduced by kind permission of the Oxford University Press. Figure 3.4 from Bateson, P. P. G. and Wainwright, A. A. P. (1972) 'The effects of prior exposure to light on the imprinting process in domestic chicks', *Behaviour*, 42, 279–90. © 1972 E. J. Brill. Used with permission. Figure 3.6 from Horn, G., Bradley, P. and McCabe, B. J. (1985) 'Changes in the structure of synapses associated with learning', *Journal of Neuroscience*, 5, 3161–8. Reproduced by kind permission of the Oxford University Press. Figure 3.7 from Johnson, M. H., Bolhuis, J. J. and Horn, G. (1985) 'Interaction between acquired preferences and developing predispositions during imprinting', *Animal Behaviour*, 33, 1000–6. © 1985 Bailliere Tindall. Used with permission. Figure 3.8 Used by kind permission of the artist, Priscilla Barrett. Figure 3.10 Used by kind permission of the artist, Priscilla Barrett. Figure 4.1 from Kleiner, K. A. (1987) 'Amplitude and phase spectra as indices of infant's pattern preferences', *Infant Behavior and Development*, 10, 49–59. Reprinted with permission of the Ablex Publishing Corporation. Figure 4.2 from Bateson, P. P. G. and Reese, E. P. (1969) 'The reinforcing properties of conspicuous stimuli in the imprinting situation', *Animal Behaviour*, 17, 629–99. © 1969 Bailliere Tindall. Used with permission. Figure 4.3 from Bolhuis, J. J., Johnson, M. H., Horn, G. and Bateson, P. P. G. (1989) 'Long-lasting effects of IMHV lesions on social preferences in the domestic fowl', *Behavioral Neuroscience*, 103, 438–41. © 1989 by the American Psychological Association. Used with permission.

1

Why bring Biology into Cognitive Development?

There are many ways of thinking about development. The type of questions asked often depend on the discipline from which the questions come. *Cognitive psychologists* emphasize the need for information-processing accounts of children's behaviour at different ages. They are, however, less concerned either with identifying which components of their models are sensitive to environmental influence, or with identifying those factors in the social environment which facilitate the development of the child. Traditionally, the *ethologist* interested in behavioural development is keen to tease apart the nature and nurture components of behaviour patterns and to place development in its evolutionary context. The ethologist, however, is often not inclined to extend the analysis further to specify the information-processing components which might underlie the behaviours under study. A third discipline, *neuroscience*, places the emphasis on describing changes in, and identifying causes for, the development of the brain. With a few exceptions, little serious thought is given to the information-processing consequences of these changes. Yet another approach to development focuses on the identification of aspects of the social environment that influence the developing young, the *social perspective*, but this is often to the neglect of the physiological and psychological changes which undoubtedly occur within the young organism.

We will argue in this first chapter that a cognitive approach to understanding behavioural development is essential, but that a traditional cognitive approach in isolation is, at best, inadequate. To take one extreme example, if a behavioural change were *solely* dependent on the maturation of a neural structure or pathway, then attempting a cognitive account of the processes underlying this change would not only be unnecessary, but also may actually be misleading.

Of course, an information-processing account of the behaviour before and after the change would still be informative. However, there need be no account of the change itself in terms of such psychological factors as learning, insight or induction.[1]

Since each discipline offers its own particular view of behavioural development, we intend to use concepts and evidence from all of them in our study. This does not mean that we are going to attempt an explanation of development at all levels, only that an adequate account at one level (cognitive) requires some recourse to the others. Our aim in this book is to provide an information-processing account of an aspect of behavioural development. That is, our goal is to produce an account of the mechanisms that lie midway between behaviour and its neural basis. This information-processing account will, however, be heavily influenced by relevant biological and social factors.

The Cognitive Approach to Development

The cognitive approach to studying the mind and its development contrasts particularly with *behaviourism* and *eliminative reductionism*. *Behaviourism*, in its various guises, maintains that we should be interested only in observable behaviour. *Eliminative reductionists* believe that we should account for mental activity solely in terms of neural activity[2] and that there is no psychology other than 'folk psychology'. While we shall argue for the importance of taking neural information seriously in cognitive theorizing, we maintain that psychological theorizing, where the brain is described at a *functional* level, is a valid and useful scientific activity.

Our motivation for wanting to describe the brain at a cognitive level is precisely because this is the level at which humans (and other 'higher' animals) interact with the world. We comprehend sentences, paragraphs and narratives, not particular sound patterns. We identify and manipulate objects, not collections of atoms or patterns of reflected light. We enjoy our favourite food, not a collection of complex macromolecules, vitamins and trace elements. In other words, our brains have evolved to interpret the external world at a certain level. And this level is different from that at which more primitive species such as the sea slug, *Aplysia*, operates. *Aplysia* responds to a world of sensations, not of objects. Thus, although a study of such species may inform us about the cellular biochemistry of the brain, they are unlikely to be a useful model for the understanding of the human brain at a *functional* level. Regardless of our increasing knowledge of the mechanics of the brain, therefore, a cognitive approach to understanding the human mind will always be necessary.

Focusing on the internal processes that underlie behaviour, rather than on the behaviour itself, leads the cognitive psychologist to adopt a rather different view of the human mind from that of the behaviourist, especially with regard to development. The behaviourist is more inclined to view the infant's mind as an unstructured *tabula rasa*, with general principles underlying all aspects of behaviour. On the other hand, the cognitive psychologist is relatively more inclined to view the infant's mind in terms of inbuilt, dissociable and specialized computational mechanisms sometimes referred to as 'modules'.[3] The balance between inbuilt and learned behaviour, and the search for an appropriate framework within which to discuss this balance, will concern us throughout this chapter.

The problem with taking a behaviourist view of development can be seen clearly when we try and account for phenomena such as that commonly referred to in the cognitive development literature as a 'U-shaped curve'. U-shaped curves are defined in terms of behaviour: a child is able to perform a task successfully at one age and then goes through a period of being unable to perform the task before returning again to successful performance. For example, Annette Karmiloff-Smith has studied a task which involves children attempting to balance various kinds of symmetrical and asymmetrical wooden blocks on a wedge. This task is successfully performed by children between the ages of four and six, and children over eight years.[4] Children between six and eight, however, show a striking inability to find the centre of balance of an unevenly weighted rod. It is difficult to see how one could account for these data in terms of a single underlying mechanism that gradually acquires information about the characteristics of the physical world. Karmiloff-Smith, however, adopting a cognitive approach, was able to account for this U-shaped developmental sequence elegantly in terms of the development and manipulation of theories about the physical world that are held by the children.

Later in the book, in the context of face recognition, we will return to the issue of U-shaped curves in development, and argue that, at least in infancy, they are often indicative of more than one mechanism underlying the development of an ability.

Limitations of the Cognitive Approach to Development

In the previous section we discussed the importance of taking a cognitive approach to development. There are, however, a number of ways in which we feel that the typical cognitive approach to development can be, at best, inadequate or, at worst, misleading. Our first point concerns the source of metaphors commonly employed by cognitive psychologists. Since, as characterized earlier, they are interested in dissociating components of the mind, cognitive psychologists understandably look to other complex information-processing systems for analogies.[5] In practical terms, this usually means borrowing analogies from the digital computer. While this might be perfectly appropriate for theories focusing on the steady-state adult mind, difficulties arise when studying development simply because computers don't develop. As a result, the developing child is often conceptualized in terms of a succession of steady states. The mechanisms of change get neglected. We take the straightforward view that since biological organs like the brain *do* develop, we need to use metaphors that embody change itself. Thus, analogies such as those derived from neural development may turn out to be more fruitful as we attempt to characterize the *process* of change underlying behavioural development. One consequence of this is that sometimes the cognitive mechanisms we propose in this book may look a little different from those that often appear in books on cognitive development.

Our second point regarding the limitations of the cognitive approach to development also focuses on the mechanisms of change, and concerns the view that psychological development can be studied entirely in isolation of the postnatal maturation of the brain. We can illustrate the dangers of this view with an example studied by Adele Diamond and Patricia Goldman-Rakic: Piaget's A-not-B error.[6] In this task, infants watch a toy being hidden in one of two wells or under one of two cups. After a delay of several seconds the infant is allowed to reach toward where she thinks the toy is. From an early age, infants will reach to the appropriate location. If, however, after a number of trials of this kind the experimenter, in full view of the infant, switches the side on which the toy is hidden, infants younger than ten months will continue to reach toward the original location.

It is clear that a psychological account can be given of the error. Such an account might be that the infant's response is driven by her representation of the previous successful response, rather than being computed from her memory of where the object is currently hidden. But what is of interest to us at the moment is the infant's change from being in a state where errors are produced under certain experimental conditions, to being in a state some days later where the error is no longer produced under those conditions. How are we to account for the change itself?

Many developmental psychologists have spent considerable time and effort attempting to account for this particular developmental change in terms of cognitive mechanisms. Diamond and Goldman-Rakic, however, have marshalled evidence from developmental neuroanatomy, neuropsychology and the behaviour of other primates, to propose that this particular developmental change can be accounted for by the maturation of regions of the prefrontal cortex. By this view, a development at the neural level can give rise to a change in cognitive mechanisms.

Note the contrast between giving a neuroanatomical account of the infant's representations at either state and giving a neuroanatomical account of the cause of the change from one state to another. A neural account of a steady state is a different level of description from a cognitive one and may or may not be useful depending on the issue being investigated. The neuroanatomical account of the *change* of states, on the other hand, can be the appropriate cause of the change at many levels, and there need be no correct psychological account of the change. That is to say, in certain cases psychological change may be caused by a neural factor – such as the maturation of particular neural circuits.[7]

Our final point concerning the limitations of the cognitive approach is, again, a theme that will recur throughout the book. It is to take the external environment of the young animal more seriously. This becomes important when the cognitive scientist argues for a dissociation between two or more mechanisms on the basis of one of them being 'innate'. The term 'innate' is often contrasted with the term 'learning', and the emergence of any cognitive structure not attributable to learning is labelled 'innate'. One problem with this analysis is that it is very coarse, since it turns out that there are many different ways that a mechanism can be 'innate' by this definition. In other words, there are many more levels at which environmental input can influence the emergence of cognitive structures than just by 'learning'. Another problem with the usual distinction between 'innate' and 'learned' is that it invokes a rather static view of the mechanisms labelled 'innate', leaving little room for subsequent influence by aspects of the environment. Later in this chapter we return to this issue and argue for the value of dissociating different levels of environmental influence.

Biological Approaches to Cognitive Development

Having sketched out the importance and limitations of the cognitive approach to studying development, we now outline and discuss two of the areas in which biological[8] evidence has been utilized to inform debate about cognitive development. The first of these concerns the so-called 'nature–nurture' debate, while the second concerns ways that evidence on brain growth has been used to elucidate aspects of behavioural development.

The 'Nature–Nurture' Debate

The study of ontogeny, the development of the individual, was guided for many years by the framework erected by the early ethologists, most notably Niko Tinbergen and Konrad Lorenz. They and some of their followers analysed behaviour and its development into 'innate' and 'acquired' components and introduced a range of different putative mechanisms such as sign stimuli, fixed action patterns and the hydraulic model of drive states. The use of such concepts resulted in a dramatic explosion of our knowledge in this field.

As knowledge increased it became evident that there were very few, if any, examples of strictly 'innate' behaviours, that is, behaviours totally unaffected by any environmental factors. For example, Gilbert Gottlieb found that mallard ducklings, which had not previously heard any adult calls, preferred their own species-specific parental call. This preference was measured by seeing how strongly the duckling ran toward the source of a particular sound. At first sight this preference seemed like a clear example of an innate behaviour. This conclusion was strengthened by an experiment in which mallard ducklings were given extensive experience of a model emitting a wood duck call. This experience did change the ducklings' behaviour, but only to the extent that they preferred the wood duck and mallard calls equally. The 'innate' preference for the mallard call was still as strong as the learned preference for the wood duck. More recent work, however, has shown that preference for the mallard call is actually affected by ducklings' experience prior to hatching. Specifically, the ducklings need to hear the 'contact-contentment' call which they themselves make in the shell during the day before hatching. This call is unlike any adult calls. It is sufficient for them to hear their own calls for the species-specific preferences to develop. However, if they are deprived of even this experience, then the species preference is very weak or non-existent. So the auditory predisposition is dependent upon specific, but unrelated, embryonic experience.[9]

Such examples have led to an increasing disillusionment with the traditional dichotomy, and with the consequence that most researchers in the field consider themselves to be 'interactionists'. Unfortunately 'interaction' is too often treated as an answer or explanation, rather than as a statement of the problem.[10] In addition, blanket statements about interactionism do not allow us to capture many interesting differences between developmental pathways. For instance, we would want to distinguish between the fact that some behaviours in some species seemingly arise spontaneously in the absence of specific information from the environment and remain resistant to subsequent environmental changes, whereas others are acquired following relevant specific input from the environment and stay highly sensitive to environmental influences.

These issues have recently been discussed in a much-cited book by Susan Oyama.[11] This author argues cogently that the nature–nurture dichotomy is partly the result of the scientific need to think in dichotomies, and partly the result of addressing the wrong question. She maintains that the current scientific approaches to development are more deeply influenced by cultural traditions than we think. That is, both religion and science have looked for a source of prespecified instructions (information) outside the developmental process itself. While religion has attributed the emergence of structure or form to an outside creator, science has eventually decided that the source of prespecified instructions is in the gene. The first scientists interested in ontogeny hypothesized that a completely formed being existed within the 'germ', either the egg or the sperm. In both varieties of the theory, the other partner's contribution was said merely to diffuse into the preformed being. One of these preformationist theories, spermism, is illustrated in figure 1.1. Gradually, as scientific knowledge proceeded, the prespecifications for form became enclosed within the genetic material. In recent years, ever more elaborate metaphors have been

Figure 1.1 *Drawings such as this one influenced a 17th-century school of thought, spermists, who believed that there was a complete preformed person in each male sperm.*

devised as it becomes clear that the majority of genes cannot do the job of regulating development in isolation. The orchestration of development is now supposed to be controlled by 'switching' genes, but these in turn are regulated by other 'switching' genes leading us, Oyama states, into a infinite regress. While there has been much debate among those concerned with whether the genes act as a blueprint, hypothesis generator, program, code, plan or set of rules for development, no one has yet proposed that all of these views might be wrong, maintains Oyama.

In understanding development we should be concerned more with change than with the steady state, with the process not the phenotypic state at any point in time.

Nativism and empiricism require each other as do warp and weft. What they share is the belief that information can preexist the processes that give rise to it. Yet information 'in the genes' or 'in the environment' is not biologically relevant until it participates in phenotypic processes. Once this happens, it becomes meaningful in the organism only as it is constituted by its developmental system. The result is not *more* information but *significant* information.[12]

What are the implications of these arguments for the study of cognitive development? Oyama urges us not to focus on constancy during development since this inevitably leads us to look for an injection of pre-existing information from either the genes or the environment to account for changes. With few exceptions, this focus on constancy is a characteristic of models of cognitive development. This is partly because it is simply easier to describe particular stages in development than to account for the dynamic processes of change, and partly because of influential logical arguments such as those put forward by Jerry Fodor.[13] Fodor argues, for example, that it is impossible to learn a language of thought whose predicates express extensions unexpressable in the previously available language. By Oyama's view, Fodor's arguments are based on a very static and stage-like conception of development. The emergence of a new language of thought should not be attributable to either learning or maturation (the latter of which Fodor settles for), but should be seen as a product of the preceding developmental system. Despite the obsession of some of his followers with particular *stages* of development, perhaps only in Jean Piaget's original writing is there an attempt at least to address increases in significant information as part of the developmental process itself.[14]

Unpacking development: species-typical and individual-specific environments

If we take the interaction arguments seriously then we must inevitably lose some of our traditional tools of analysis. While we take the criticisms of interactionists such as Oyama to heart, we are unaware of any alternative framework that would allow us to unpack develop-mental sequences clearly and easily.[15] Thus, there is an impasse: accepting the interaction arguments mean that we lose some of our ability to analyse development. We propose that a way out of this interactionist impasse is to separate out distinct classes of environmental influence on phenotypes. Instead of the dichotomy being reduced to environmental input versus no environmental input, we put forward a framework which distinguishes between the various levels of environmental input.

As far as we can see there are at least three levels at which 'environment' interacts with genotype. First, there is the environment within the genetic material. The location of a gene in the genetic material will determine when it is expressed, and with which other genes. Second, there is the local biochemical environment which can either act with gene products, or act upon the gene itself. Third, there is the interaction between the product of the first two levels and the world outside the organism. It is only this latter level of environmental influence that is directly relevant to those interested in cognitive development. From here on we shall use the phrase *internal environment* for the first two levels of environmental influence, and *external environment* for the latter. At the level of the external environmental input we propose another distinction, that between the *species-typical environment* (STE) and the *individual-specific environment* (ISE).[16] To illustrate this distinction let us return to the duckling example once again. The preference for the mallard species call only developed when the embryo was exposed to a particular (unrelated) auditory input at a particular stage. Since this particular input is common to all normal members of the species, it would be characterized as being part of the STE. Further learning about a particular adult bird's call, an experience unique to an individual, would be part of the ISE.

Within this framework we will use the term *primal* to refer to any cognitive mechanism that results from the interaction between the animal (even before birth or hatching) and any non-specific aspect of its species-typical environment. Note that structures arising following specific information from the species-typical environment (learning) would not be classified as being *primal*. This definition will be expanded upon in the light of particular examples to be given in chapter 3. Gottlieb's example of the mallard ducklings, discussed on pages 6–7, would involve *primal* structures since the environmental trigger that resulted in a species-specific preference was a sound that bore no relation to the adult call subsequently preferred by the chicks. We reiterate that, by this analysis, something can only be *primal* with *respect to particular level of interaction with the environment*. This use of the word *primal* therefore, does not equate with 'genetic' or with the traditional use of the term 'innate'.[17] We also wish to reserve the phrase 'developmental system' for the interaction at the level of the species-typical environment. Thus, any given species will have a normal 'developmental system' or pathway which is the product of the interaction at the level of the internal environment and the STE.[18] Any individual that deviates from this pathway is, by definition, classified as abnormal.

It is important to note that some aspects of the environment can act as both STE and ISE for the same species. For example, the language input to a human child provides both STE and ISE. Language input itself is species typical, and any language input[19] will serve to develop some language-specific structures of the brain. In this sense all languages are equivalent. At the same time, the particular language we hear as an infant is part of the ISE. Such an analysis can be carried further by identifying particular aspects of the grammar that are part of the STE. Note that even if certain aspects of grammar turn out to be universal to all cultures, this does not mean that it is 'genetic'. It does suggest, however, that it is part of the human developmental system. Whether or not it is *primal* would depend upon how specific the environmental triggers have to be. In box 1.1 we outline the implications of this framework for our understanding of individual differences within a species.

The Developing Brain and Behaviour

A second way in which information from biology has been brought into the study of cognitive development has concerned the influence of postnatal brain maturation. The study of the role of brain maturation on behaviour goes back to at least 1926 when Carmichael demonstrated in a series of experiments with young frogs that the onset of swimming is dependent upon age rather than experience.[20] Another example of early work in this area was the work of Wendell Cruze on pecking accuracy in chicks.[21] Cruze established that pecking accuracy in the chick matured over the first five days of life regardless of the amount of experience that each bird was allowed. Most of the early work on human infants also concerned the development of motor skills. For example, one experiment took advantage of the ancient Hopi Indian tradition of strapping their infants to a cradle board for the first nine months of life.[22] A group of Hopi infants raised in the traditional manner were compared to a group of Hopi infants allowed to move

Box 1.1   Sources of individual differences

The distinctions we have made between the two kinds of environment help to eliminate another confusion, that among various
sources of individual differences within a species. We would want to
point to at least four alternatives:

1 *Differences brought about by 'normal' variations within the
   genotype.* In humans, such differences give rise to the range of
   colour, body type and some characteristics of the central nervous
   system which lead to differences in speed of processing. This is
   the kind of variation that is usually referred to when the phrase
   individual differences is used. 'Normal' variations in lower-level
   environments (especially the *in utero* environment) would be
   functionally equivalent here. Thus, maternal variations in diet
   would shift the average height without affecting the genotypic
   variation.
2 *Abnormal variations within the genotype.* Down syndrome would
   be one such variation. (Though we might note that the decision to
   term such variation 'abnormal' has a strong cultural component).
   Again, we have the functionally equivalent environmental variations
   such as thalidomide, with its well-known consequences. Another
   example is maternal rubella, which, in combination with genotypic
   factors, can lead to autism.
3 *Violation of the species-typical environmental – STE.* We envisage
   that the STE will include aspects of the environment such as the
   presence of light and objects in the visual world, auditory
   stimulation, the presence of conspecific caregivers, etc. More far-
   reaching cases of violation would be blindness and deafness. Such
   conditions would lead development down different tracks –
   though the extent of this is still unknown. Some of the supposed
   effects of deafness, for example, are brought about by the lack of
   early language input, rather than by deafness itself.
4 *Variations in individual-specific environment – ISE.* The ISE will
   include aspects of the environment unique to an individual or
   group of individuals. The clearest case of variation is the language
   community within which we are raised. That the authors both call a
   spade a spade rather than *une polle* is simply due to this. The
   nature of a child's upbringing also affects intellectual development.
   Thus, variation in IQ, as commonly measured, is clearly an
   outcome of the interaction of the genotype with the ISE.

freely like infants from other cultures. The age of onset of walking was found to be identical in the two groups (15 months). Other studies conducted in the 1930s and 1940s were more interventionist in nature. Dennis and Dennis[23] somehow persuaded a mother to lend them her new-born twins for nine months. During this time the infants were kept lying on their backs with their hand movements restrained, without toys and with no opportunity to interact with each other or with their caregivers. Despite this deprivation, smiling, cooing, sitting and grasping all emerged at around the normal time in both twins. Gesell and Thompson[24] made more use of the experimental possibilities that having twins as subjects allow. In their study one twin was given practice at an emerging skill, climbing stairs for example, while the other was denied it. Although the less experienced infant was initially slower to climb stairs on subsequent testing, the effect was only short-lived and it rapidly caught up with its sibling.

Over the past 50 years or so a variety of strategies have been employed to study these issues in human and other primates. In this section we briefly consider three of these approaches, which we call *correlative* theories, *causal* theories and *system* theories. Not all examples fall easily into only one of these approaches. However, we believe the distinction to be a useful one for characterizing the general approaches taken.

Correlative theories

Since intervention is not possible in human studies, neural correlates of psychological changes are sought under this approach. Such correlates are sometimes tested using animal models or through comparisons with clinical populations. The neural correlates invoked include changes in the structure of neurones and their components, electrophysiological changes and myelinization. Modern examples of this approach include the work on the maturation of the prefrontal cortex in relation to Piaget's object permanence task and the A-not-B error mentioned earlier. The reader is referred to box 1.2 for more detailed discussion of this example.

The major problem with purely correlational accounts for developmental change is that they are *post hoc*. When this approach is combined with one or both of the other two, however, then predictions derived from the neural level can be made at the cognitive level. We

Box 1.2   Comments on the prefrontal lobe and delayed memory

Patients with brain damage in the prefrontal region have difficulty with tasks where they are required to wait for a time before responding. Such a task has also been found to discriminate monkeys with damage to the same region. Diamond and Goldman-Rakic noticed the similarity between the delayed-response test and an object-permanence test devised by Piaget which gives rise to the so-called 'A-not-B' error (see pp. 4–5). They found that infant monkeys appeared to show the same developmental progression on A not B between one and four months as human infants show between seven and 12 months.

The next question was how human infants would behave in another task shown to be sensitive to frontal cortex damage. In this simple task the subject is required to reach for an object (food item or toy). The object is in a box with transparent plastic walls, except that one of the side walls is open. An earlier study had shown that monkeys with frontal damage will only reach straight for the food and will consequently fail. Diamond found that infants of six–seven months were also unable to retrieve the reward. However, by 11–12 months infants were successful at the task. The younger infants, then, behaved very much like the brain damaged adult monkeys, leading to the conclusion that the developmental changes seen in the infants can be attributed to the maturation of the frontal cortex rather than being the product of learning. There are, however, a number of issues, both specific and general, which require discussion before the results can be interpreted in this way.

The specific problem relates to some of the assumptions which underlie this example. In the object-permanence task the proficiency of infants is assessed by the time delay required before they make an error. This delay increases steadily between seven and 12 months. It is claimed that the increase correlates with frontal cortex maturation. This step in the reasoning presupposes two things: first, that the structure matures in a gradual manner and second, that the physiological basis of this maturation must allow information to be retained for a gradually increasing length of time under the conditions of the task.

One general problem concerns what constitutes a brain region. Most parts of the brain appear to be involved in one or more circuits and Goldman-Rakic herself has suggested that the frontal cortex is part of a circuit which includes other areas of the cortex as well as subcortical regions. Damage to one part of the circuit would impair the functioning of the whole circuit. Equivalently, the maturation of a circuit will depend upon the state of development of its slowest link. It is at least conceivable that damage to the frontal region merely mimics immaturity of the entire circuit and that the actual structural developments responsible for the behavioural changes lie elsewhere on the circuit.

There remains the problem as to the psychological function which these maturing circuits are purported to be supporting. Diamond and Goldman-Rakic came to the conclusion that the prefrontal cortex is necessary whenever a representation requires to be retained over a period of time (Diamond and Goldman-Rakic, 1983). However, Jean Mandler has shown that infants of 11 months have no problem in retaining information for periods of up to a minute (Mandler, 1988). It is apparent that the prefrontal function, which leads to the decline of the A-not-B error, is not necessary for Mandler's task. Thus, even though the developmental anatomy is responsible for giving rise to the change, we still need a separate psychological characterization of what has changed.

shall see some examples of this combination of approaches later in the book.

Causal theories

This approach is concerned with elucidating the prerequisites essential for normal, and especially abnormal, psychological development. Causal arguments are often based on the influence of such factors as hormones and neurotransmitters on developmental sequences.

Perhaps the best known recent example of the kind has been proposed by Norman Geschwind and Al Galaburda. In brief, their proposal is that there is a causal relationship between aspects of the endocrine environment *in utero* and the development of cerebral dominance, and a possible further relationship between the former and the immune syndrome. The embryological migration of neurones from the neural crest to the cortex is thought to be under the control of testosterone. Higher or lower levels of testosterone were postulated to slow down or accelerate the maturation process thereby bringing about abnormal cortical organization. A consequence of this, Geschwind and Galaburda proposed, could be the defective development of the left cerebral hemisphere, which in turn could account for the association between certain developmental disorders and (a) the very strong male predominance and (b) the higher rate of left-handedness than the general population. The disorders that Geschwind and Galaburda suggest they can account for include dyslexia, stuttering, autism and hyperactivity.

An argument such as this depends on many causal links. In box 1.3 we discuss in more detail the evidence for the components of the theory and the logic with which they interrelate. In general, however, it is sufficient to point out that any such causal theory that purports to give rise to a variety of outcomes also has to give an account of why one outcome, rather than the others, should occur in any particular case. That is, the Geschwind–Galaburda theory could give, at best, only a non-specific account of a prerequisite for dyslexia or autism.

Note, however, that the motivation of the Geschwind–Galaburda theory was to create a causal link from a hormonal abnormality, through a resulting neuroanatomical deviation, to a behavioural disorder. The difference between this approach and the correlational approach mentioned earlier, is that in the latter the abnormal neuroanatomy would simply be presented as a correlate of dyslexia.

Box 1.3   Comments on the Geschwind and Galaburda theory

The theory described rests on a number of assumptions. Even if one accepts that testosterone is a regulator of brain development and that maturation is associated with hemispheric specialization, one is left with the problem as to why, in the theory, only the left hemisphere becomes abnormal. There are two reasons for such an asymmetry which might be proposed:

1 Testosterone acts specifically on the left hemisphere.
2 Testosterone has its effects only at a certain stage in development. The right hemisphere develops more slowly than the left and it could be that the hormone reaches the crucial levels at a time when the left hemisphere is vulnerable and the right is not; the hormone drops to safe levels before the right hemisphere has reached the same stage as the left. Since boys have a higher incidence of dyslexia and autism than girls, the greater vulnerability of the male foetus still has to be fitted into this picture.

In either case we have the position that the failure of the left hemisphere to develop normally results in various 'developmental learning problems'. Taken in a strong form, this stage of the argument is obviously inadequate, leaving no account of why one child turns out dyslexic and another autistic. One possible form that the argument could take is that left-hemisphere underdevelopment is one of several prerequisites for these disorders. For each of the disorders there would have to be at least one unique prerequisite. Another option is that because of other sources of variation, different infants suffer left-hemisphere damage in different locations, each one corresponding to a different developmental disorder. Note that even if either of these alternative claims were true, the causal route which Geschwind and Galaburda describe – faulty cell migration leads to developmental disorders – would in no sense be defining for any particular one of these disorders.

An alternative view of the data is that left-hemisphere abnormalities, rather than being the cause of autism, are merely a correlate or, indeed, a consequence of the condition. Some support for the latter status may be derived from the fact that adult schizophrenics may show similar disorders of hemispheric specialization. As yet the evidence is not sufficient to decide between these causal alternatives. Nor do we have measurement of testosterone levels *in utero* to establish whether there are cases of children with abnormal testosterone levels who do not suffer from such developmental disorders.

One problem with the theory is that cause has been confused with prerequisite. Cause, for us, implies a unitary outcome. This obviously is not the case in the strong versions of the Geschwind–Galaburda theory, for several different disabilities are a possible consequence of the same thing.

System theories

This general strategy is concerned with devising algorithms or rules to represent changes in states at both the neural and cognitive level. Since these are theories about dynamic rather than static systems, the type of evidence required to support them is more difficult to obtain. Research usually proceeds by attempting to derive rules for change of states at either the neural or the cognitive level before an attempt is made to apply it to the other.

As mentioned earlier, theories of cognitive development are generally more concerned with describing the successive steady states through which a child may go. We suggested that this is at least partly because there is no appropriate source of analogy from which the child developmentalist can borrow. One of us (Johnson) has recently explored the extent to which alternative accounts of neural development may be useful for characterizing change at the cognitive level.[25]

A common observation made by those studying the development of nerve cells and their connection in the brain is as follows. Initially, nerve cells grow and migrate to a particular region. Following this the nerve cell will grow an axon and many dendrites. These processes, in turn, will grow many synapses, the transmission junctions with the processes of other cells. So far everything accords with a naïve notion of development. However, in the next stage of development a substantial portion of the synapses, processes and cells die away.[26]

Recently, several contrasting theories have been put forward to account for these observations. For example, Jean-Pierre Changeux and his collaborators from Paris have proposed that connections between classes of cells are specified 'genetically', but that these connections are initially labile. Synapses in their labile state may either become stabilized or regress, depending on the total activity of the post-synaptic cell. The activity of the post-synaptic cell is, in turn, dependent upon its input. Initially, this input may be the result of spontaneous activity in the network, but rapidly it is invoked by environmental input. The critical concept here is that of *selective stabilization*. As Changeux says, 'to learn is to eliminate'. As well as the general version of the theory presented here, Changeux has also provided a mathematical expression of the model and a detailed biochemical account of the factors determining process death. In figure 1.2. we illustrate the general principle behind Changeux's theory.

A similar, although less formally specified theory has been put forth by Sven Ebbesson.[27] He proposes that a process, which he refers to as *parcellation*, is important in both ontogenetic and phylogenetic development. Evolutionary pressures have resulted in the selective loss of connections and cellular aggregates in an initially fairly undifferentiated vertebrate brain. This selective loss results in the isolation of particular circuits and neuronal aggregates from others, and the increasing differentiation of the brain. According to Ebbesson a similar process occurs during ontogenetic development.

Note that, within the framework for environmental influence discussed earlier, both theories attribute the initial over-production of

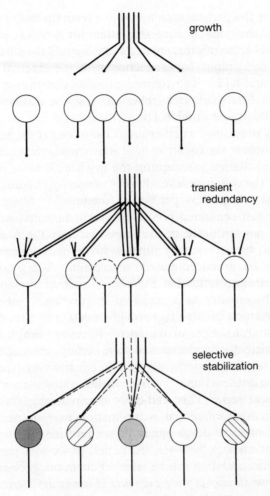

growth

transient
redundancy

selective
stabilization

Figure 1.2   *A schematic representation of the process of selective stabilization. An initial stage of growth followed by the elimination of redundant connections. From Changeux (1983).*

connectivity to interactions at the level of the internal environment. The selective reduction of this connectivity, however, is attributed to the external environment by Changeux and to the internal environment by Ebbesson[28] (since the same process underlies phylogenetic development).

A further distinction has been made by Johnson, with regard to the stage at which there is a reduction of connections.[29] This distinction is to dissociate the particular *pattern* of loss from the *timing* of the loss. In particular, the idea is that the extent of loss of connectivity is determined by the internal environment whereas the particular pattern of loss is determined by interaction with the external environment (both ISE and STE). The Johnson proposal constitutes an alternative to those of Changeux and Ebbesson, and the distinctions between them are illustrated in table 1.1.

One way to enquire whether such distinctions at the neural level can be informative at the cognitive level is to investigate whether processes such as parcellation can capture the essence of some developmental changes at the cognitive level. Recent notions of cognitive functioning suggest that we possess perceptual 'modules'.[30] These modules are held to be self-contained processing units. Information within these modules is encapsulated in the sense that only the final output of a module can be accessed by other systems. Any intermediate stages which may be produced remain inaccessible. While some cognitive developmentalists hold that modules are either present at birth or appear subsequently as a result of maturation,[31] others hold that cognitive systems become increasingly modular as a result of development.[32] As an example of the latter, Karmiloff-Smith has proposed that at a particular developmental stage certain syntactic structures are accessible to other systems. By adulthood, however, the system may become encapsulated and the information contained within it can no longer be accessed.[33] This, and other examples, suggest that a process of increasing informational encapsulation may occur during some aspects of cognitive development. What remains unclear at present is how far the analogy between the neural process of parcellation and cognitive encapsulation can be taken. For instance, clear examples of encapsulation *through a process of selective loss* at the cognitive level have yet to be presented.

Table 1.1 The level of environmental influence on the reduction of neuronal connectivity

Connectivity reduction	Changeux	Ebbesson	Johnson
Timing	external	internal	internal
Pattern	external	internal	external

If extended to the cognitive level, all three accounts of loss of neural connectivity yield different predictions with regard to the issue of patterning and timing in cognitive development. For example, while both the Ebbesson and Johnson accounts predict a maturationally timed end to sensitive periods, the Changeux account does not. The end of the sensitive period is taken to correspond to the stabilization of the particular neuronal group. In the Changeux model, this would be determined by the external environment input. In the other two accounts it would be determined by internal factors. With regard to these predictions, evidence from second-language learning indicates that it is the age of first exposure, rather than the number of years of exposure to a second language that predicts final proficiency.[34] The reader is referred elsewhere for more detailed discussion of these issues.[35]

Why Study the Development of Face Recognition?

Neither author is interested in face recognition for its own sake. We embarked upon the research programme described in this book, and the book itself, in the belief that this was an ideal area in which to begin to investigate how information from biology could be used more seriously to influence theories of cognitive development. While we are by no means alone in maintaining that evidence and ways of thinking from several disciplines are required for a complete account of development, with a few notable exceptions this belief has rarely been put into practice. Focusing on the development of face recognition in human infants, we hope to begin to provide one such account.

The survival of the young of many species, including our own, depends on their being able to recognize others of their own kind. As we shall see, in different species different mechanisms and strategies for solving this problem have evolved. We will compare and contrast the mechanisms underlying species recognition and its ontogeny in several species. The psychological level mechanisms which have evolved in species can be seen to be the result of a variety of selective pressures. For example, the precise requirements upon the system for species recognition, at different stages of infancy in any species, will depend upon the social environment and the ecological niche into which the animal is born, in other words upon aspects of its species-typical environment (STE).

We shall go on to analyse in detail the mechanisms underlying the development of conspecific recognition in two species which have been studied extensively, the domestic chick and the human infant. It has been shown that, soon after hatching, the chick is predisposed to attend toward objects with certain characteristics possessed *inter alia* by adult hens. A learning system is then engaged by the features of objects to which the young bird is attending. If these two systems are combined with an appropriate natural environment (STE), the chick will learn the characteristics of its own mother.

Our experiments on human infants suggest that roughly analogous systems may be at work. From birth, babies are prepared to move their head and eyes further to keep a face in view than they are to keep various 'scrambled' faces in view. We will argue that this behaviour is controlled by a simple orienting mechanism, possibly mediated by subcortical structures. Following the maturation of the primary visual (cortical) pathway at about two months after birth, a new mechanism becomes available. This mechanism allows the infant to learn the detailed characteristics of the human face in general, and those of its mother, or other caretaker, in particular. This developmental sequence in the human infant provides an example of psychological change for maturational reasons. In addition, the idea of two interacting mechanisms serves to reconcile some long-standing contradictions in the literature on infant face recognition.

2
The Development of Face Recognition

Human faces are particularly interesting to other humans. Indeed, we often 'see' faces in the moon, in the clouds and even when we stick three pieces of coal and a carrot into a ball of snow. Psychological experiments have revealed that our ability to process information about faces is greater than for any other class of visual stimuli. A typical experiment showing this to be the case involves a subject deciding which one of two pictures matches a third. Sometimes the pictures are all the right way up and sometimes they are all inverted. When the pictures are inverted, subjects are normally slower and less accurate in this matching task than when the pictures are the right way up. The degree to which the subjects are affected by the inversion, however, depends upon whether the pictures are of faces or of some other commonly observed class of visual stimuli such as houses. If the pictures are of faces, subjects are more accurate to start with but are about 25 per cent less accurate with inversion. In contrast, with pictures of houses, for example, inversion would decrease accuracy by only 10 per cent or less. This differential effect of inverting stimuli became known as the 'inversion effect' and was regarded by many as strong evidence that unique processing mechanisms underlie face recognition. This mechanism was conceived of as being so specialized that it could deal only with upright faces, not inverted ones. The possibility remained, however, that subjects simply have more experience with faces than with any of the other classes of visual stimuli investigated. In order to test whether the 'inversion effect' is really specific to faces or whether it results from a great amount of experience with any class of visual stimuli, one would have to study a class of stimuli that had been examined very closely and for a prolonged period by experienced subjects.

Recently, Rhea Diamond and Susan Carey at Massachusetts Institute of Technology set out to test this hypothesis by using dog-show judges to match pictures of dogs[1] (see figure 2.1). They found that when the dog judges were tested with breeds other than that which they were qualified to judge or when they had been judging a breed for only a few years, they did not show a strong inversion effect. When very experienced judges were asked to perform the task with individual champion dogs of their specialist breed, however, a strong inversion effect similar to that obtained with faces was found.[2]

The fact that it took the dog judges many years of experience of judging a breed before they developed an inversion effect is of great interest, since Susan Carey and others had earlier found interesting changes in the way that faces are encoded even quite late in childhood.[3] This, and other evidence, suggest that the adult humans' expertise in processing faces is exactly that: an expertise effect resulting from observing the details of faces for decades, rather than the product of a unique and specialized mechanism for processing faces. This leaves open the question of how such expertise develops in the first place. To answer the question we must go back to the first few days and weeks of life.

Introduction to the Development of Face Recognition

Psychophysical studies of infant vision have suggested that the amount of information obtainable from a face in early infancy is very limited. For example, some authors[4] argue that a one-month-old infant may be able to discern only the grossest features of the face: the outer contour defined by the hairline and vague darker areas in the region of the eyes and mouth (see fig. 2.2). A related claim about the visual capacities of infants in the first two months of life is that they attend to the boundaries of stimuli in preference to the interior – the so-called 'externality effect.'[5] This factor, taken together with the supposed limitations in sensitivity previously mentioned, lead to the expectation of poor face recognition abilities in infants under two months.

Since infants cannot talk to tell us about what they know, various techniques have been developed to ascertain the extent of their knowledge non-verbally. Many of these techniques utilize the tendency of young infants to look toward interesting visual stimuli (see box 2.1). With regard to infants' knowledge about faces, most studies have

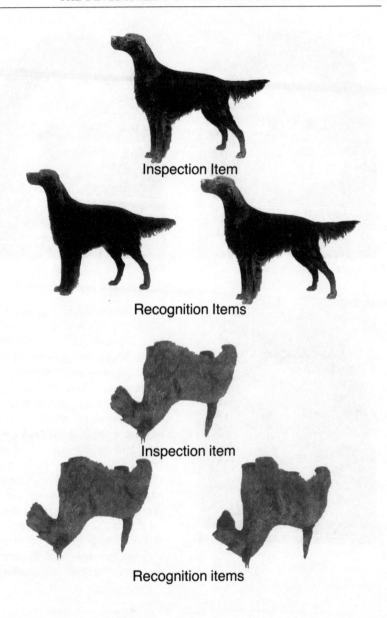

Inspection Item

Recognition Items

Inspection item

Recognition items

Figure 2.1 *Examples of the stimuli used by Diamond and Carey.*

The effect of infant's limited acuity. These photographs simulate viewing of a life-sized face at a distance of about 50 cm. with a degree of optical blur that removes detail (high spatial frequencies) beyond the infant's acuity limit. (a) sharp image, (b) blur removes all spatial frequencies beyond a three month-old's acuity limit and (c) blur removes all spatial frequencies beyond a one-month-old's acuity limit. The remarkably small loss of useful visual information in (b) and even in (c) depends on the short viewing distance; high acuity is principally important for distance vision, or for very fine manipulative skills and reading.

Figure 2.2   *A face as 'seen' by infants of one and three months of age.*

Top left: figure (a); top right: figure (b); bottom left: figure (c).

involved showing infants pictures of faces and other stimuli of interest and measuring the extent to which the infants look at the face pattern as opposed to the other stimuli. Using techniques such as these, a number of experimenters have tried to determine the age at which infants have knowledge of the correct arrangement of features that compose a face.

In general, experimenters have used schematic faces for these experiments rather than real faces. There are a number of reasons for

Box 2.1   How to make a baby talk

Most experiments with infants rely primarily on two facts. The first is that, other things being equal, infants prefer to look at something familiar rather than something totally new. The second fact is that after looking at anything for a while, infants get bored. The technical term for this is *habituation*. The next time they are shown the same stimulus they look at it for a shorter period of time. The familiarity preference can be seen as a long-term effect and the novelty preference as a short-term effect.

Some experimenters get their infant subjects to work to amuse themselves. The best technique for this is called non-nutritive sucking. The baby is given a dummy which is connected to a device that registers when the baby is sucking. A computer counts the sucks and arranges for the baby to be shown a stimulus or to be played a sound. The stimulus continues for a little while and then stops, unless the baby continues to suck. As time goes on the baby gets bored and the rate of sucking drops.

With both these techniques one can tell how interested a baby is in a particular stimulus by measuring its initial response. After the baby has habituated one can find out what they have learned about the first stimulus by playing or showing a second stimulus which has been altered from the original in a particular way. If the baby still seems bored then we know that it has not noticed the change in the stimulus; if the baby becomes interested again we know that it has noticed the change. We call this effect, the novelty discrimination, *dishabituation*.

All the experiments we have carried out, on human infants or on chicks, have relied on familiarity preference. From time to time, however, we will discuss the work of other people who have used the habituation–dishabituation technique.

this. In the first place, black and white schematic stimuli are easier for the infants to see than photographs. Second, if we use real faces there is always the problem of keeping good control over what it is that the infant sees. Real people have difficulty keeping their faces still and control stimuli are not easy to devise. Because of this, it is not evident how to ask questions about what the infant really knows. If we use schematic faces, it is easier to get clear answers from the infant. Note that since new-born infants prefer looking at bold schematic drawings of faces rather than real faces, we are unlikely to underestimate their abilities. On the contrary, we are giving them every chance to show us what they know.

In table 2.1 we summarize some of the available evidence concerning the age at which infants first show a preference for a schematic face over a schematic 'scrambled' face. The latter type of stimulus is usually made up of the pieces of a face arranged in a different way. These stimuli are used because they share with the face a number of characteristics which have been believed to influence infants' attention. These properties include the number of elements, the total amount of black–white boundry and the total area of black.

With one exception, to which we will return, authors have claimed that it is not until two or three months of age that infants first show a preference for the normal schematic face. One of the most cited studies supporting this view is that conducted by Daphne Maurer and Marie Barrera at McMaster University.[6] These authors used a testing procedure which was known to be very sensitive to young infants' preferences in order to establish whether one- and two-month-old

Table 2.1 The ages at which various studies have first detected a preference for a schematic face over various types of symmetrical scrambled face patterns

0	1 mo.	2 mo.	3 mo.	4 mo.
Goren, Sarty and Wu 1975		Maurer and Barrera 1981	Fantz 1966 (assymetric)	Wilcox 1969 Kagan et al. 1966 Sigman and Parmalee 1974 Fantz and Nevis 1967

Source: Adapted from a fuller table in Maurer, 1985

infants had a preference for a schematic face as compared to a scrambled schematic face. In this testing procedure, the experimenter presents a slide of one of the stimuli to the infant. The slide is presented for as long as the infant looks at it. When the infant looks away, the slide is turned off. The length of time that the infant looks at the slide is recorded and then the next slide is presented. The process is then repeated for all the test stimuli, with each stimulus being presented at least twice in a counterbalanced, random order. The technique is thought to be very sensitive, since it is the infant itself who terminates each bout of looking.

Maurer and Barrera found that while two-month-old infants looked for significantly longer periods at the face-like configuration, the infants of one month of age did not. This result suggests that it takes a couple of months of exposure to faces for infants to learn about the correct arrangement of facial features. When similar, but less sensitive, testing procedures are used then a preference for the face-like pattern is not found until three or four months of age.[7]

In the research we have summarized up to now, there is agreement that infants do not respond differentially to faces until they are at least two months old. Evidence such as this led Eleanor Gibson to provide what quickly became the prevailing view of the development of face recognition. To cite Gibson herself:

> Development takes the course of first responding discriminatively with crude compulsory fixations on high contrast edges or spots in the field. Then follows gradual extraction of distinctive features of the oft-presented face object, differentiated as individual features only. Later comes noticing of invariant relations between features such as the two eyes in a given orientation in the head; later still, the array of features characterising a real face as distinct from a dummy's or from schematic drawings is distinguished, with no one feature any longer dominant.[8]

The theme here, followed by many people since, is that of a gradual acquisition of individual elements and their spatial relationships.

Accounts such as that of Gibson seem very plausible and parsimonious. However, more than a decade ago Carolyn Goren and her colleagues[9] published the results of a study that examined the way new-born infants (median age nine minutes) tracked a moving schematic face, scrambled 'faces' or a blank head outline. Their results were quite clear: measures of the extent of head and eye movements indicated that there was stronger interest in the face pattern than in the other stimuli.

The result of this study, indicating that babies only a few minutes old preferentially attend to faces, is clearly in conflict with the findings discussed earlier. It was not surprising, therefore, that these findings remained largely ignored by psychologists despite their far-reaching theoretical implications.[10] It was easy to accept that one-month-olds did not show a preference while two-month-olds did, since it could be assumed that sufficient learning had taken place by the latter age to allow a perceptual representation to be formed, or that it is only by two months that infant vision is sufficiently developed to resolve the details of a face. The results obtained with new-borns, on the other hand, suggest that infants enter the world with some considerable perceptual 'knowledge'. Furthermore, we have to explain why several studies involving infants of one month of age and younger failed to find a preference for a schematic face over a scrambled face.

This pattern of results, with a preference for faces at birth and at two months but not at one month is, at first sight, odd. If it is correct, it would seem to make untenable accounts of the development of face preference purely in terms of gradual learning or in terms of the steady maturation of a single neural structure. Since some authors had pointed to possible methodological flaws in the original Goren study, attempts to replicate and extend both this and some of the other studies are clearly required.

Replication of Goren, Sarty and Wu[11]

We were just about to begin an attempt to replicate the Goren et al. experiment when we discovered that such an attempt was already being conducted by Suzanne Dziurawiec and Hadyn Ellis at the University of Aberdeen.[12] The Aberdeen study included a number of improvements in the methods of data collection during the experiment, which ensured that no unconscious bias on the part of the experimenter could influence the results.[13] The sample consisted of 24 normal, healthy new-borns who were tested within the first hour after birth. The stimuli employed were three head-shaped, head-sized, two-dimensional white forms, about 17×19 cm., with black features of a human face, as used by Goren and colleagues. In figure 2.3 the stimuli, referred to as *Face*, *Scrambled* and *Blank*, can be seen. The experimenter shuffled the stimuli and presented them approximately 18 to 25 cm. from the infant's face. The experimenters were entirely unaware of the order of presentation of stimuli during testing since

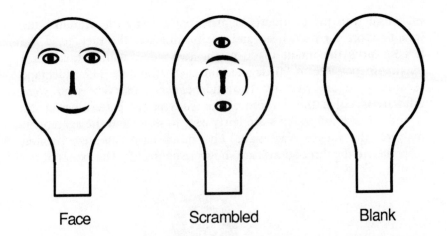

Face   Scrambled   Blank

Figure 2.3   *The three stimuli used in the replication of Goren, Sarty and Wu.*

only the identical and unmarked reverse sides of the stimuli were visible to them. Illumination of the stimuli was provided primarily by natural light from a very large window situated above and behind the infant.

Each infant was placed on its back on the experimenter's lap and surrounded by a large protector over which the stimuli were to be presented against a light-coloured ceiling seven feet away. The infant reclined on thick towelling, with its neck supported by the experimenter's palm beneath the towelling. The arrangement of the experimenter and infant is shown in figure 2.4. The baby's head was aligned mid-line with the 0-degree mark on the protractor and the first stimulus, randomly selected, was positioned directly in front of the baby's face. As soon as the infant fixated the stimulus, it was moved slowly to one side along the arc of the protractor, at a rate of approximately five degrees per second. If an infant responded with a head turn or an eye turn greater than 60 degrees it was tested to the other side.[14] If the infant failed to turn or turned only minimally, up to seven attempts were made to elicit a satisfactory turn to that side. The procedure was then repeated to the opposite side. The next stimulus, also randomly selected, was then used. Finally the third stimulus was used. The infant's eye and head turning in pursuit of the stimulus were recorded on videotape for later analysis. As in the Goren study, the extent of following, measured in terms of degrees of arc, was determined by comparing the final nose position and eye orientation on each trial with the protractor demarcations. For each stimulus, the infant's score for both head and eye turning was the average of the largest turns the infant made to the two sides, with a theoretical maximum possible of 90 degrees for each stimulus. The videotape records were analysed by two independent observers who were unaware of either the purpose of the study or the patterning on the stimuli. These judgements are fairly easy to make and the agreement between the judges was high. The mean head- and eye-turning responses to the three stimuli are shown in figure 2.5. The extent of the

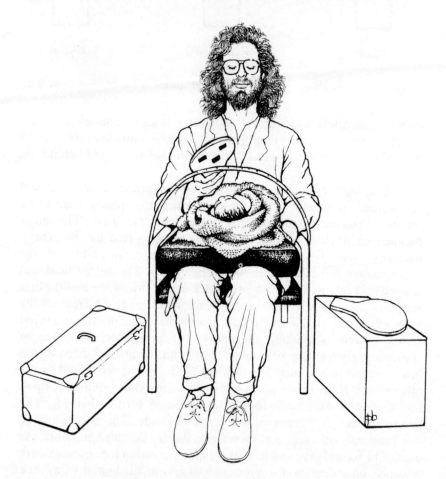

Figure 2.4 *The arrangement of experimenter and infant in the replication of the* Goren *et al.* study. Drawing by Priscilla Barrett.

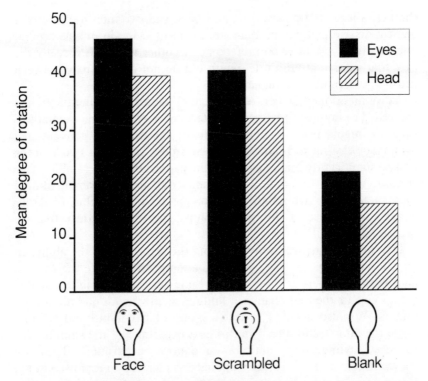

Figure 2.5   *Mean head and eye turning for the real, scrambled and blank face stimuli. The face is followed significantly further than the other stimuli.*

eye turns to the *face* were significantly greater than those to the *scrambled face*, which, in turn, were greater than those to the *blank* stimulus. The same differences were found by measuring the extent of head turning.

The results obtained by Dziurawiec and Ellis clearly replicated the findings of Goren and her colleagues. Neonates do appear to attend more strongly to patterned stimuli than to a head shape with no internal features. Most importantly, a face-like pattern elicits a greater extent of tracking behaviour than does a non-face-like pattern.

Replicating the Data Concerning Infants of One and Two Months of Age

Now that we have more confidence that new-borns do show a discriminatory response toward a face-like pattern, we can move on to the next piece of the puzzle. If new-born and two-month-old infants show a discriminatory response toward faces, why do infants around one month of age have no preference? In other words, is it really the case that infants around one month old do not discriminate between intact and scrambled schematic faces?

As we mentioned earlier, only Daphne Maurer and colleagues[15] had succeeded in finding a preference for faces over symmetrical 'scrambled' faces in infants prior to four months of age using the conventional preference testing techniques. In their study, infants of two months looked significantly longer at a face-like pattern than at scrambled-face stimuli, whereas one-month-old infants did not. Maurer attributed their success with two-month-olds, compared with the failure of earlier work, to their use of the 'infant-control' testing procedure that we described earlier.[16]

Due to the controversy surrounding the age at which the ability in question first appears, we decided to attempt to replicate the Maurer and Barrera experiment using the same testing technique, as this would give us the best chance of finding an effect with one-month-old infants. We also decided to test a group of five-month-old infants, using the same technique.[17] In this next experiment[18] the stimuli were life-sized, white, head outlines on a grey background. They are shown in figure 2.6. The *face* stimulus was identical to that used in the Goren experiment and its replication. Another stimulus, *config*, possessed the configuration (arrangements of stimulus elements) of a face without the details of facial features. We will discuss the

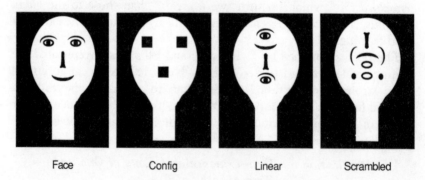

Face   Config   Linear   Scrambled

Figure 2.6 *The four stimuli used to test infants' preferences in the attempt to replicate the Maurer and Barrera study. All stimuli were life-sized white, head outlines on a grey background.*

significance of this particular stimulus in more detail later in the book. The third stimulus, *linear*, was similar to one of the scrambled faces used in the Goren study, while the fourth stimulus, *scrambled*, had neither the arrangement of elements that compose a face nor intact facial features. This last stimulus served as a general control to assess the infants' baseline length of looking at a complex monochromatic pattern.

The babies sat on their mothers' lap, around 90 cms from a rear projection screen. For each trial in the experiment, we first attracted the infant's attention to the screen, either with a flashing red light or by tapping on the screen from behind. Once the infant was looking in the right direction, we displayed one of the four stimuli on screen by means of a slide projector. The experimenter watched the infant on a video monitor and switched off the slide when the infant looked away. For the entire experiment the infant's head and eye movements were recorded on videotape, and the length of time that the infant had looked at each slide was later assessed by a person who was unaware of which particular stimulus was being presented. This is an important step in the procedure, which ensures that no unconscious bias on the part of the experimenter can influence the final results.

Figure 2.7 shows the mean length of time that infants in the three age groups looked at each of the four stimuli. There were no significant differences between the times spent looking at the four stimuli for the one month of age group. In contrast, for the infants at two months of age, the *face* was looked at for significantly longer than any of the other stimuli. With the five-month-old group there were significant differences among the four stimuli, but these were not in the expected direction. In this subject group, 12 out of 15 infants looked at the *face* for shorter periods than each of the other three stimuli. We will explore this finding in more detail in chapter five. For the time being, however, we may simply conclude that infants of five months discriminate between the face and the other stimuli.

In common with Daphne Maurer and other experimenters we were unable to find any evidence that infants of one month respond to the general characteristics of faces. The mean looking times of around 20 seconds correspond closely to those found in her earlier study.[19] The two-month-old group showed significant preferences among the four stimuli, looking most at the intact *face* (Indeed, one infant stared at the face for over three minutes before looking away!). Again, this result replicates the findings reported by Maurer and her colleague. We also

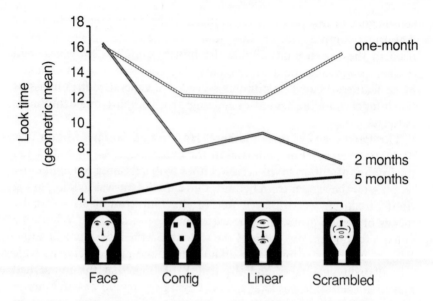

Figure 2.7   *Geometrical mean look times for each of the four stimuli at each age group. For both the 2-month-old and the 5-month-old groups there was a significant effect of stimulus on mean look time.*

extended the earlier findings by showing that, for the two-month-old group, the preference is not just for a face-like configuration, but that features of a face must be present in their correct locations. Three high-contrast elements in the correct relative spatial arrangement for eyes and a mouth, are not sufficient stimulus at this age.

At the beginning of this chapter, in our brief review of the existing literature on the development of face recognition, we described apparently contradictory bodies of evidence. New-borns and two-month-olds preferred faces to scrambled stimuli but the infants of one month of age did not. It was important that both sets of evidence should be replicated. This has now been done. We now know that there is a real problem for the existing theories of the development of face recognition.

In chapter one we pointed out how it was difficult for theories, which assume a single mechanism, to account for developmental U-shaped curves. In this chapter we have established that, while new-born infants and two-month-old infants prefer to look at faces, infants around one month old do not. In other words, we have what appears at first sight to be a U-shaped developmental curve. It is difficult to see how to account for the pattern of data observed in terms of gradual increases in perceptual abilities or learning. In the next chapter we turn to evidence from biology in an attempt to begin to provide a more satisfactory explanation.

3

Bringing in Biology

Ethology involves the study of the phylogeny and ontogeny of the behaviour of whole organisms in their natural environment. The emphasis is on how the whole brain or mind of an individual member of a species comes to function successfully within a particular environmental niche. This is in contrast to much of cognitive and neuro-science where particular mechanisms, regions or pathways are studied without a great deal of consideration as to how they relate to the natural environment and to the behaviour of the whole organism.[1] Such differences in emphasis become particularly important when considering development. This is due partly to some of the problems mentioned in chapter one in identifying the appropriate mechanisms of change. That is, new information in a developing system is rarely the exclusive product of the environment or a particular brain system, but usually involves some interaction between a number of brain systems with aspects (species-typical or otherwise) of the natural environment.

The Evidence from Ethology: the Ontogeny of Conspecific Recognition

In order to obtain protection and food, young animals of many species are required to recognize their mother or some other conspecific caregiver shortly after birth or hatching. Some species depend primarily on sensory modalities such as smell or hearing for their recognition. We shall provide some examples where the visual characteristics of the caregiver are recognized, and will focus on illustrating the range of such abilities found in vertebrate species.

Some species, for example the cuckoo, must have rather specific mechanisms for recognizing conspecifics. Within a very short period of time (about ten seconds) the cuckoo hen lands in the nest of a host species, ejects one existing egg, and lays her own (often a cuckoo copy of the host species egg, similar in colouring, speckling and size).[2] Different groups of cuckoos specialize in parasitizing different species of host. When the cuckoo chick hatches out it looks quite different from its nest mates. The cuckoo is initially without feathers and is much larger than the feathered chicks of the host, such as reed-warblers. In some strains of cuckoo the chicks' beak and mouth parts resemble those of their nest mates, but even when they do not the host parents will dutifully feed the cuckoo chick. The cuckoo chick does not go on to behave like a reed-warbler or dunnock for the rest of its life, however. After leaving the nest it goes off to mate with, and behave like, other cuckoos. Cuckoo visual conspecific recognition may therefore be mediated by *primal* structures.

Other species do not get the opportunity to learn about the characteristics of their parents for different reasons. The hornbill mother plasters herself up in a tree trunk to lay her eggs. The tree hollow must be securely plastered up to ensure that egg-eating snakes and other predators do not get in. Therefore, the chicks hatch out in a confined, secure place with little or no light. After hatching, the mother pecks a small hole in the plaster through which the father passes food items for the first few weeks. With no predators and no light there seems little purpose or possibility for the young hornbill to learn to recognize its mother by visual cues. Once the young hornbills are old enough they peck their own way out of confinement. Not surprisingly, they start begging for food from any species of bird that happens to be passing. Presumably, since the young hornbills can fly by now, they can escape from aggressive encounters with adult birds of other species.

The Birds and the Bees

The question of how species recognition develops has been experimentally studied by the use of cross-fostering experiments in certain avian species. In these cross-fostering experiments, the male young of one species is raised by parents of another species. When adult, the sexual preferences of these birds are assessed. This is often done by putting the sexually mature male in a cage with two females in cages at each side. The experimenter then observes the direction in which the

male directs his behaviour, such as singing. If it prefers the species with
which it was raised over a member of its own species then it is said to
have learned about the characteristics of this species in early life. In
contrast, if it prefers its own species despite its early rearing, then it is
supposed that the information on which it bases its sexual preferences
does not require early experience. This technique was pioneered in
Bielefeld, Germany by Klaus Immelmann and his collaborators who
studied two closely related species of finch, zebra finches and
Bengalese finches. Immelmann showed that zebra finches raised by
Bengalese finches directed more of their adult sexual behaviour
towards the foster species than did normally reared birds. This
preference occurred even if the bird was separated from its foster
parents before it began to show any sexual behaviour and appeared to
be fairly stable throughout the bird's adult life. Because the information
appeared to be acquired early in life and was stable once acquired, the
term 'sexual imprinting' came to be used. In addition to the preference
arising from early experience, Immelmann considered that there was
an unlearned preference bias for own species. The fostered zebra finch
still showed some interest in other zebra finches on first viewing. The
normally reared zebra finch, however, showed little or no interest in
Bengalese finches.

In recent years, experiments by Carel Ten Cate, of the University of
Groningen, have established that the unlearned preference or bias for
own species reported by Immelmann depends upon certain aspects of
the zebra finches' species-typical environment.[3] For example, in one
experiment it was established that there are differences in the style of
parental care between Bengalese finch and zebra finch adults. Zebra
finch parents seem to engage in more contact behaviour (including
aggression) toward their young than do Bengalese finch parents.
Experimentally reducing the extent to which a zebra finch parent can
interact with a male chick reduces the 'own species bias' of the zebra
finch chick considerably.[4] Furthermore, the extent to which a
Bengalese finch parent interacts with a zebra finch chick is positively
correlated with that chick's subsequent preference for Bengalese finch
adults. It appears, therefore, that the 'own species bias' of the zebra
finch is particularly sensitive to an aspect of the zebra finch species-
typical environment, namely that its parents engage in many aggressive
encounters with it. Note that during the preference test the male was
not allowed to interact physically with the females. The preference
could not, therefore, have been determined by such factors as the

female zebra finch behaving in an aggressive fashion reminiscent of the parents. Accordingly, we may say that the mechanism underlying this discrimination in male zebra finch chicks is *primal* by the definition described in chapter one (p. 10).

Species and Individual Recognition in Non-human Primates

What do we know about the mechanisms underlying the recognition of kin in primates other than man? In 1980 a startling paper appeared in the journal *Nature*. Gene Sackett and his colleagues from the Regional Primate Center at Madison, Wisconsin, claimed that young rhesus macaques preferred to approach half-siblings which they had not seen previously over completely unrelated rhesus macaques which they had also not seen previously.[5] This result indicated that there was a preference for kin independent of experience. If kin recognition could take place without early experience, then species recognition may follow as a consequence of this.

Unfortunately, however, subsequent attempts to replicate this result have been unsuccessful. Indeed, more recent experiments by Sackett and his collaborators have indicated the overriding importance of early experience for the recognition of individual conspecifics in later life. For example, Fredrickson and Sackett[6] compared the preferences of young rhesus macaques among unrelated–unfamiliar, related–unfamiliar, unrelated–familiar, and related–familiar individuals. Familiarity was found to be the sole basis for preference, while relatedness was unimportant.

Other studies have tackled the question of species recognition more directly. Sackett and Ruppenthal[7] report an experiment on three infant pigtail macaques. These animals were separated from their mothers at birth and raised in wire cages as 'partial isolates'. This means that while in these wire cages they had no physical contact with other monkeys of any age, but the infants could see, hear and smell pigtail and rhesus age mates. When the infants were still under two months old they were given the opportunity to approach three cages in which there was an adult pigtail female and adult females of two other species of macaques, stumptail and rhesus. The partial isolate pigtails all strongly preferred the female of their own species. Separately, one stumptail baby reared in a similar manner was tested at 1.5 months of age, and was the only infant to prefer the stumptail female. Since the pigtail and stumptail infants were raised with equal experience of rhesus infants and their own species, it seems likely that they have a *primal* mechanism underlying preference for their own species. That is, the preference of stumptails and pigtails for their own species does not depend on specific experience of the visual characteristics of conspecifics.[8] Similar experiments were carried out by Swartz,[9] also at the Wisconsin Regional Primate Centre. Rather than use preference for live models, however, Swartz used a 'habituation–dishabituation' procedure with pictures of three macaque species. Young pigtail macaques (three weeks old), reared in partial isolation with their own species as described above, discriminated between pictures of adult pigtail macaques and adults of two other species.

Sackett and Rupenthal also tested a number of rhesus macaque infants. These too were reared as partial isolates, but since they were only able to see other rhesus infants, we cannot tell whether their subsequent preference for the rhesus female over stumptail and pigtail females was due to learning in infancy or due to a *primal* mechanism. Rhesus macaque infants have also been studied at the Primate Research Institute in Kyoto, Japan, in work involving foster rearing.[10] The experiments conducted in Japan provide evidence that if there is a *primal* mechanism in the rhesus, it can be overidden following rearing by a closely related species, the Japanese macaque. In contrast to the findings with rhesus, Japanese macaque infants prefer their own species even when raised by rhesus parents. That is, their *primal* preference for their own species cannot be overriden, even by extensive experience of another species. Why might there be this assymmetry? It appears that Japanese macaques often live in mixed social groups with other species of monkey, making it necessary for these macaques to be able to identify their own species from a very young age. In contrast, rhesus infants are raised in troupes that rarely intermingle with other primate species. Thus, the specificity or otherwise of the information provided by the species-typical environment may determine the robustness or specificity of the *primal* mechanisms concerned with conspecifics. When both sources of information are combined, recognition of the own species results.

At what stage are the characteristics of the individual mother learned? Although this question has not been examined directly, evidence from experiments where very young rhesus infants (between one and five days old) were taken from their own mother to a different individual rhesus mother have indicated that the infants respond to their adopted mother in a different way from normal infants even many months later.[11] This may have been due to early learning about their original mother. Such early learning may be 'guided' by the *primal* mechanisms discussed earlier.

To conclude, the evidence we have reviewed from non-human primates and other species suggests that the young recognize the features of their mother as a result of experience of her, and that this learning may take place even over the first few days of life. Recognizing their own species, however, appears often to be the result of a combination of the species-typical environment and the *primal* mechanisms of the neonate. In species where their species-typical environment includes exposure to the characteristics of several species (such as the Japanese macaque), the *primal* mechanisms possessed by the neonate may be more specific and are even able to survive the prolonged exposure that results from being reared by a different species.

The Ontogeny of Face-sensitive Neurones

Given that primates appear to have sophisticated face processing abilities, it seems reasonable to enquire into the neural basis of these abilities. Several research groups throughout the world are interested in particular groups of neurones which are found in the temporal lobe of rhesus macaques that appear to respond more readily, or more vigorously, to the presentation of faces than to a variety of other complex visual stimuli (see figure 3.1).[12] These neurones, found in distinct 'clumps' within the superior temporal sulcus (a part of the temporal lobe), may respond to different aspects of a face. Some neurones respond maximally to a particular individual's face, some to particular elements or views of a face only and some to other monkeys only or to humans only. One obvious question is whether some of these neurones are responsive to aspects of faces from birth or whether their selective responsivity is a product of exposure to faces either during infancy or during adult life.

Due to the technical difficulties involved in trying to carry out such experiments with young monkeys, these questions have only just begun to be investigated. Hilary Rodman and Charles Gross at Princeton University attempted to make recordings from face-specific cells in the temporal lobe of young monkeys. After several years of work on this project the youngest monkey that they have been able to

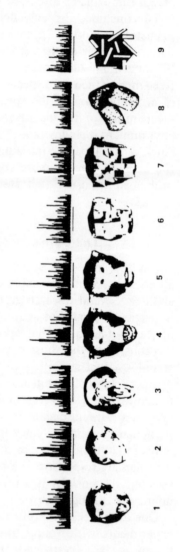

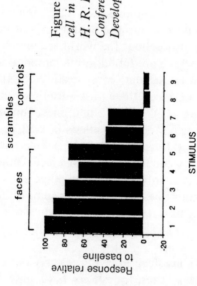

Figure 3.1 The response of a typical 'face-sensitive' cell in the macaque temporal lobe. Adapted from H. R. Rodman (1989) paper presented to the Biennial Conference of the Society for Research in Child Development, Kansas City, KN.

find evidence of face cells in was six weeks of age.[13] Unfortunately, since we do not yet have reliable data on younger monkeys we cannot conclude that the specificity of any of these cells is present from birth. Indeed, six weeks corresponds well with the age of rapid cortical maturation in the infant monkey[14] so it may be that these cells gain their specificity through exposure to faces over the first few weeks of life.

In some informal pilot experiments conducted in collaboration with Dave Perrett at St Andrews University, one of us (Johnson) used, with day-old rhesus monkeys, some of the testing techniques described earlier which were designed for use with human infants. Although very preliminary, some tentative evidence was found for a preference to attend toward intact 3-dimensional rhesus monkey face models as opposed to similar models with scrambled features. Whether such a preference is based on the activity of superior temporal sulcus neurones, or of some system elsewhere in the brain, remains an open question. This finding is consistent, however, with the evidence in support of some *primal* mechanism supporting species preferences in rhesus.

Perhaps a more promising approach toward the systematic investigation of early rearing environments on face-sensitive cells will be the study of such cells in sheep. Keith Kendrick and colleagues, working near Cambridge, have been studying the properties of similar cells in the sheep temporal lobe.[15] As in the macaque, some cells in the adult sheep respond to faces of animals of the same breed, some to individual sheep, some to humans and dogs and some to the length and shape of horns (see figure 3.2). By studying the effects of rearing lambs with non-horned mothers, Kendrick hopes to be able to investigate whether the sheep require experience of horns for horn-sensitive cells to become specifically responsive to that stimulus.

Imprinting and the Development of Conspecific Recognition in the Chick

In the absence of a mother hen, newly hatched chicks will approach a wide range of bright or moving objects. After a period of exposure to such an object they form a social attachment to it. When they are close to the object the chicks emit soft 'contentment' calls and if the object moves away they will follow it. If subsequently exposed to a new object

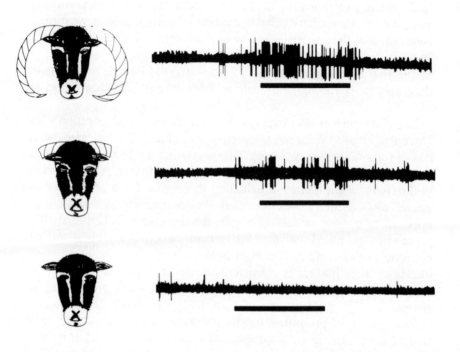

Figure 3.2 *The response of a typical 'horn-sensitive' cell in the sheep temporal lobe. From Kendrick (1990).*

the chicks will run away from it while emitting 'distress' calls. From these observations it may be inferred that chicks learn about some of the visual characteristics of the first conspicuous object to which they are exposed. This process is referred to as filial imprinting, and has been studied more intensively in precocial birds such as domestic chicks, ducklings and goslings.[16] Box 3.1 describes and discusses the original claims about imprinting made by the famous Austrian ethologist, Konrad Lorenz.

Imprinting in domestic chicks can be reliably reproduced in the laboratory in the following way. Chicks are dark-reared until they are exposed to a conspicuous object such as a rotating, illuminated red box for a period of time, normally from one to three hours (figure 3.3 shows some typical objects used in imprinting experiments). From between two hours to several days later, chicks are given a preference

Box 3.1   Comments on the original claims of Konrad Lorenz

Many experimental investigations of imprinting have been concerned with testing the validity of the claims originally made by the Austrian founder of ethology Konrad Lorenz. Briefly, Lorenz (1937) made three claims:

1   *Imprinting is confined to a short well-defined period in the life-cycle, the critical time or period.* Lorenz claimed that if exposure to an object did not take place within a particular critical time period a preference would not be acquired. This period was thought to be delineated by endogenous changes only. More recent evidence suggests that the period is less rigid than Lorenz supposed and may only come to an end once the initial object can be discriminated from the surrounding environment and other objects. For example, chicks that have been reared in darkness for several days will imprint as strongly as those exposed to an object on the first day of life (Johnson, Bolhius and Horn, unpublished) Imprinting has thus come to be viewed as a self-terminating process (see Sluckin, 1972a).

2   *Imprinting is irreversible.* Jaynes (1956) pointed out that Lorenz's claim about the irreversibility of imprinting could be interpreted in either of two ways: once a bird has become imprinted on an object it will never again address its filial responses to dissimilar objects or, alternatively, it may come to address its filial responses to dissimilar objects but always retain information about the original object. Over the years a considerable amount of evidence has accrued to suggest that imprinting is not irreversible in the first sense (see box 3.6 and chapter four for more details).

3   *Imprinting normally involves learning the characteristics of the species rather than those of an individual member of the species.* Originally, for Lorenz the function of imprinting was '. . . to establish a sort of consciousness of species in the young bird'. This assertion led to the assumption that learning about an individual takes place by 'normal conditioning' (Hess, 1959). Evidence in this chapter indicates that imprinting is involved in learning about the individuals rather than the species.

Figure 3.3   *Examples of objects which have been successfully used as imprinting stimuli. All of the stimuli are illuminated and rotate; (a) and (b) are translucent and illuminated from within by a coloured bulb. Scale bar = 10 cm. After Horn (1985).*

test in which they have a choice between the object to which they were exposed and a novel object. In general, chicks prefer to approach the object which they have seen previously. The more closely two objects resemble each other, the less preference chicks show for the one seen previously. It is assumed, then, that the relative preference for different objects gives us an index of what the chick has learned, or already knows, about the objects in question.

It is possible to quantify a chick's preference for one object over another by recording the extent to which it approaches the two objects. In some preference tests the familiar object (seen during the training session) and the novel object are presented at the same time, one at each end of a runway (see figure 3.4). The extent to which a chick approaches each of the two objects over a certain time period, usually five to ten minutes, is recorded. In another type of preference test the familiar and novel objects are presented sequentially, one after the other. Again, the extent to which a chick approaches each of the two objects is recorded. After the end of a preference test a 'preference score' may be calculated. One commonly used preference score is as follows:

$$\text{Preference score} = \frac{\text{Approach toward the familiar object}}{\text{Approach toward the familiar} + \text{the novel objects}}$$

This preference score, the approach toward the familiar object divided by the total approach toward both objects, is multiplied by 100 in order to obtain a percentage figure for any given chick. Commonly, a mean preference score is calculated for a group of chicks in an experiment.

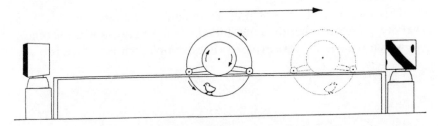

Figure 3.4 *A diagram of one preference test that involves showing both the familiar and the novel objects at the same time, the 'Railway test' devised by Bateson (1972). The wheel is geared so that the chick recedes from the object it tries to approach.*

It is important to note that the preference score is independent of the overall activity of the chick. This makes it a clearer measure of learning than simply taking the magnitude of approach toward the familiar object as a measure of imprinting. If we took only this latter measure then chicks who were generally more active would score higher than chicks who happened to be less active. It is vital, therefore, that we always compare the chick's preference for the familiar object to its preference for a novel one, and use a measure independent of overall activity such as the preference score defined above.

The Neural Basis of Imprinting

Using training and testing techniques such as those described above, Gabriel Horn and Patrick Bateson at the University of Cambridge have investigated the neural basis of imprinting in the domestic chick. Many neural theories of memory suppose that a particular experience or event leads to the formation or strengthening of pathways in the brain through changes in the size or number of contacts between nerve cells.[17] Reasoning that such changes may be associated with protein synthesis, Bateson and Horn collaborated with a biochemist, Steven Rose, to study the uptake of precursors of protein synthesis into different large regions of the chick brain after imprinting.[18] These precursors assist in the process of building proteins, and the extent to which they are used up in a given area was taken to correspond to the amount of new proteins being produced. The only region where there was a higher incorporation of these precursors in the imprinted chicks, as compared to non-imprinted controls, was in a region referred to as the forebrain roof (see figure 3.5).

This increased uptake of precursors could, of course, be due to a variety of factors other than the storage of information about the object to which the chicks were exposed. For example, while a chick is being

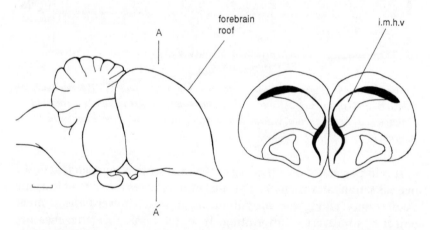

Figure 3.5   *Outline drawing of the chick brain. The brain is viewed from the side and is about 2 cm. from front to back. The vertical lines AA' above and below the drawings of the side view (left) indicate the plane of the coronal section outline (vertical slice–right) through the forebrain. IMHV = the intermediate and medial part of the Hyperstriatum Ventrale. The location of the forebrain roof is indicated.*

exposed to an imprinting object it may be more active, more 'aroused' or more attentive than a chick not exposed to such an object. In order to determine whether the biochemical changes observed could be attributed to any of these other factors a variety of control procedures were devised. One of these involved 'split-brain' chicks in which visual input during training was restricted to one side of the forebrain only.[19] Biochemical measures similar to those applied in the earlier experiments were used to study birds that learned with the trained hemisphere, but showed no learning with the untrained one. Incorporation of precursors of proteins was higher in the 'trained' hemisphere than in the 'untrained' one. If the biochemical differences had been due to some general factor such as arousal or motor activity, then the same effect should have been found on both sides of the brain.

A second experiment, conducted by Bateson, Horn and Rose, concerned the extent to which a chick learns during a training session.[20] On the day after hatching two groups of chicks were exposed to an imprinting object. One group was exposed to the object for a long enough period of time to ensure that they were strongly imprinted (the 'over-trained' group), while the other group was exposed to the object for only a short period of time, insufficient to establish strong imprinting (the 'under-trained' group). On the second day after hatching both groups were exposed to the same imprinting object for the longer period of time. The uptake of protein precursors during the second training session was measured. Despite both groups having equal visual and motor stimulation during the second training period, the 'under-trained' group (who were still learning about the imprinting stimulus) showed significantly more uptake of protein precursors than did the 'over-trained' group (who had achieved most of their learning about the stimulus on the first day). The results of these and other studies have confirmed that there is a strong relationship between the biochemical changes observed and learning.[21] Since the biochemical changes were closely tied to the learning process of imprinting it was necessary, for more detailed analysis of these changes, to enquire whether they were localized to particular parts of the forebrain roof.

A small 'sausage'-shaped region immediately around the midpoint between the anterior and posterior poles of the cerebral hemispheres, which Bateson et al. referred to as IMHV (the Intermediate and Medial part of the Hyperstriatum Ventrale; see figure 3.5) was identified using autoradiographic techniques.[22] Subsequently, the same region of

Box 3.2   IMHV and learning

Although the integrity of IMHV may be critical for tasks requiring the recognition of individual conspecifics (Johnson and Horn, 1987), it also appears to be essential for the successful performance of at least one other task which does not have this requirement: one-trial passive avoidance learning. Newly hatched chicks will peck at a wide variety of small objects when presented to them, including small coloured beads. If the bead is coated with an unpleasant tasting substance, methyl anthranilate, approximately 75 per cent of chicks will refrain from pecking on subsequent re-presentation of the bead. With birds where the bead has been coated with water, all but about four per cent will peck on subsequent presentation (Lee-Teng and Sherman, 1966). A variety of biochemical and structural changes following passive-avoidance learning have been described within areas closely corresponding to IMHV (for example, Kossut and Rose, 1984; Patterson *et al.*, 1986). Davies, Taylor and Johnson (1989) investigated whether bilateral IMHV lesions similar to those that impair imprinting, would also impair chicks in passive-avoidance learning. While intact chicks and chicks with lateral forebrain lesions, avoided the distateful bead on subsequent re-presentation, the IMHV-lesioned chicks did not. In the passive-avoidance task the chick is required to recognize the characteristics of a particular coloured bead and to associate this with its unpleasant taste. Thus, the task could be described as requiring the formation of a representation of a specific visual object. It may be that this characteristic, which the passive-avoidance task shares with imprinting, is critical to the involvement of IMHV.

co-extensive areas have also been identified by other groups studying visual and auditory imprinting.[23] If IMHV is indeed a crucial site for imprinting then damage to it prior to imprinting should prevent the acquisition of preferences, and its destruction after imprinting should render a chick amnesic. This was confirmed in experiments performed in the Cambridge laboratory by Horn and Bateson in collaboration with Brian McCabe.[24] Similar sized lesions placed elsewhere in the forebrain had no such consequences. It is important to note that localized damage to IMHV has strikingly little effect on the general behaviour of the chick. For example, such chicks still move about and feed exactly like 'normal' chicks do. Indeed, chicks with damage to IMHV are only impaired on some forms of complex learning tasks (see box 3.2 and chapter four, pp. 92–3). Since these initial experiments, the chick IMHV has become one of the most studied regions of the brain implicated in learning. The interested reader is referred to box 3.3 for further details.

Box 3.3   Neuronal changes associated with information storage

Having established that IMHV is critically involved in imprinting it is interesting to examine whether any changes take place in the structure of synapses within the region following imprinting. Horn, Bradley and McCabe (1985) under-trained one group of birds on a red box (20 minutes exposure) and over-trained another group (140 minutes exposure). A third group of chicks served as dark-reared controls. Following training, samples were taken from the IMHV of each hemisphere; ultrathin sections were cut and examined under an electron microscope. There were no differences in any measure of synapse morphology between under-trained chicks and dark-reared controls. Chicks that had been trained for 140 minutes differed from the other two groups in only one measure of the synapse structure: the mean length of the postsynaptic density (see Figure 3.6), the thickened part of the postsynaptic membrane, which had increased by 17 per cent. The change was restricted to synapses on dendritic spines (axospinous) within the left IMHV.

The postsynaptic density appears to be a site of high neurotransmitter receptor density (Fagg and Matus, 1984), so that an increase in the area of this region suggests an increase in the number of receptor sites. Following imprinting, McCabe and Horn (1988) found a significant increase in the number of sites in the left IMHV of chicks compared with dark-reared controls (as estimated by NMDA-sensitive binding). Furthermore, they found a significant positive correlation between the number of receptor sites and the degree to which a chick preferred the familiar stimulus at testing. This evidence indicated that the increase in the number of binding sites could not be attributed to visual stimulation, arousal or locomotor activity per se, but only to how much the chick had learned.

It would be reasonable to expect that the changes in synaptic structure and biochemistry described above would result in changes in the spontaneous firing of neurones within left IMHV. As a first step in analysing the electrophysiological changes in left IMHV in relation

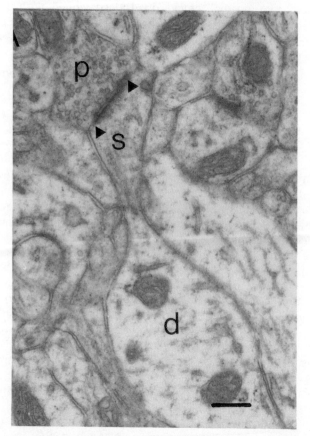

Figure 3.6 *Photomicrograph of an axospinous synapse in IMHV. The thickened membrane between the arrowheads is the synaptic density: d = shaft of dendrite; p = presynaptic bouton; s = spine connected to the shaft of a dendrite. Scale bar = 200 nm. After Horn et al. (1985).*

to training, Payne and Horn (1984) exposed chicks to an imprinting stimulus for three hours. The amount of approach that each chick made toward the stimulus during this time was recorded. After the final hour of training, the chicks were anaesthetized and the rate of firing was measured in a visual projection area (they hyperstriatum accessorium) and in IMHV. A significant negative correlation was found between total approach during exposure to the object and the mean firing rate of units within the left IMHV. One possible explanation of this finding is that the more the chick has been imprinted on a stimulus, the less spontaneous activity is recorded in

IMHV since the neural circuits 'relax' into a stable state on presentation of the familiar stimulus. There was no correlation between the mean firing rates of units in the visual projection area and approach behaviour. The electrophysiological correlates of training were thus region specific, so that the changes in left IMHV neuronal activity were unlikely to have resulted from some non-specific effects of training, such as arousal, which might be expected to affect both brain regions.

The Red Box and the Stuffed Hen

Two different imprinting stimuli were used in the ablation studies discussed above. In most of those experiments half of the chicks were trained by exposure to an illuminated rotating stuffed hen[25] and the other half by exposure to a rotating red box illuminated from within (see figure 3.3). Presented in isolation, both stimuli elicited active approach from naïve chicks, and strong preferences resulted from an hour or two of exposure to them. When reviewing a series of studies on the effects of IMHV lesions on the retention of filial preferences however, Horn and McCabe noticed that, although there were no significant differences between box-trained and hen-trained birds within any one study, taken over several studies there was a striking stimulus-dependent effect. When IMHV was damaged the preference for the red box by chicks trained on that object was very greatly reduced while the preference for the hen by chicks trained on the stuffed hen was only slightly reduced.[26] This result was interpreted as suggesting that some of the neural circuits involved in imprinting may differ according to the nature of the stimulus involved.

If different neural circuits are involved, then it is possible that these circuits could be differentially affected by biochemical manipulations such as varying hormone or neurotransmitter levels. In collaboration with Johan Bolhuis, a zoologist from the University of Groningen, McCabe and Horn[27] investigated the effect of manipulating levels of the hormone testosterone on chicks' preferences. Testosterone was investigated since it has commonly been associated with the regulation of specific aspects of behaviour in birds and mammals. They found that administration of testosterone prior to training increased the preference for the hen in birds exposed to that stimulus, but was without effect on birds exposed to the box. Furthermore, in hen-trained birds a significant positive correlation was found between plasma (blood) testosterone levels and the extent of preference for the stuffed hen. No such correlation was found in birds trained on the red box. Since it is reasonable to assume that the levels of testosterone in the blood reflect those in the brain, we may conclude that the hormone is closely associated with preference for the hen, but not for the red box.

Another biochemical manipulation that yielded stimulus-dependent effects involved a substance which has been implicated in the plasticity of the brain, noradrenaline. Noradrenaline is present in the chick forebrain and its levels increase with age and with experience of a visual imprinting stimulus during the first 50 hours after hatching.[28] Administration of the neurotoxic drug DSP4[29] depletes forebrain noradrenaline levels by about 65 per cent in the chick. Such treatment profoundly impairs the acquisition of preference in birds exposed to the red box; in contrast, birds exposed to the hen are only slightly impaired.[30] Furthermore, a significant positive correlation between preference score and noradrenaline concentration was found in a brain sample composed mainly of IMHV, but only for birds exposed to the red box. No such correlation was found for birds exposed to the stuffed hen.

Thus, while testosterone is related to preference for the familiar object in stuffed-hen-trained birds but not for the red-box-trained birds, noradrenaline is related to preference for the red-box-trained chicks, but not to birds trained on the hen. Taken together then, the noradrenaline and testosterone evidence suggest a double dissociation of function; at least part of the neurochemical substrate underlying preference for the stuffed hen differs from that underlying preference for the red box. This neurochemical double dissociation, taken together with the evidence regarding the effects of damaging IMHV mentioned earlier, provide a convincing case that exposing chicks to the stuffed hen has different neural consequences from exposure to the red box. This exciting discovery led to much discussion in the laboratory, and to even more lively debate over an occasional pint of beer in a nearby pub.[31] During one of these discussions someone recalled a proposal made many years before by Robert Hinde, that chicks may be predisposed to find certain specific characteristics of the mother hen attractive.[32] However, the problem remained that while it was already well established that chicks have non-specific preferences for certain colours and sizes of objects, no one had yet found any evidence that there are specific unlearned preferences relating to the characteristics of a mother hen and, still less, that such a specific predisposition interacts with learning during imprinting tasks. With these thoughts in mind, Mark Johnson collaborated with Bolhuis and Horn on a series of experiments to enquire into what predispositions might influence the behaviour of chicks in the context of filial preference.

In an initial experiment, day-old domestic chicks were exposed to either the rotating red box or the rotating stuffed hen.[33] Two hours or 24 hours after this period of exposure the preferences of these chicks were ascertained by simultaneously presenting both the red box and the stuffed hen to each chick.[34] As expected, when tested two hours after training, both the box-trained and hen-trained chicks preferred the object to which they had previously been exposed. However, when tested 24 hours after training both box- and hen-trained chicks showed a relative shift in preference towards the hen compared with the chicks tested after two hours. That is, the hen-trained birds had an even stronger preference for the hen than did their counterparts at the first testing time, while the box-trained birds tested at the later time had no preference for either object. These data are shown graphically in figure 3.7. Although these results, taken in isolation, could be accounted for in terms of differential forgetting, the results from a third group of chicks suggested a different interpretation. The chicks in this group were not exposed to any imprinting object prior to testing, but were merely exposed to dim overhead light at the same time as their counterparts in the other groups were being trained. While being exposed to overhead light the chicks were in individual running wheels, but could not see each other. Since birds in this group were not exposed to any object it was not surprising that they had no preference for either test object two hours after being exposed to light. Contrary to expectation, however, other birds from the same group tested 24 hours after exposure to light had a strong preference for the stuffed hen. These results reinforced the suggestion that the filial preferences of trained chicks could be accounted for in terms of the interaction between acquired preferences on the one hand, and a developing predisposition on the other.

A Specific Predisposition

As mentioned earlier, it had been known for some time that chicks have general predispositions to respond to particular classes of stimuli

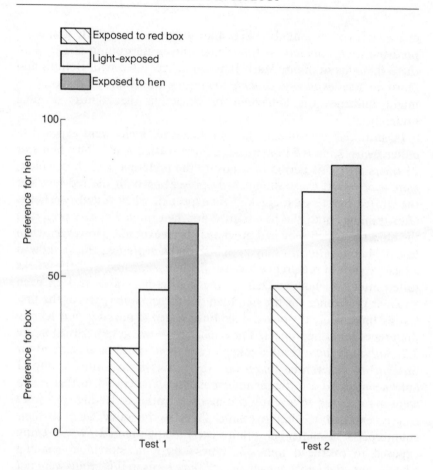

Figure 3.7   *A schematic representation of the results from Johnson* et al. *(1985).*
All mean preference scores are expressed as a preference for the stuffed hen. Plain
bars represent baselines at test 1 (2 hours) and test 2 (24 hours) set by the respective
untrained control groups.

in particular ways. For example, naïve chicks are predisposed to
approach moving objects larger than matchbox size, while they will
peck at objects smaller than a matchbox.[35] Although some authors
have suggested that more specific visual predispositions may be
operating in filial behaviour,[36] until recently no evidence for such a
specific visual predisposition had been found.

The experiment just discussed provided evidence for the existence
of a predisposition. Chicks who are not exposed to any conspicuous

object, but are merely exposed to dim overhead light for a couple of hours while in running wheels, show a significant preference for the stuffed hen over the red box 24 hours later. We may conclude that these chicks possess a preference that is not acquired through interaction with the ISE (individual-specific environment). That is, the preference is *primal* by the definition introduced earlier. As we stressed in chapter one, this does not mean that empirical investigation should cease. Indeed, two obvious questions arise from the observation just discussed: first, what are the necessary (species-typical) environmental conditions for the emergence of the predisposition and second, what are the characteristics of the stuffed hen that cause it to be preferred to the red box?

The first question was addressed in a series of experiments that looked at the effects of allowing the chick a period of time to run about. This was thought to be of interest since it was known that activity affects testosterone levels in some species[37] and, as already described, testosterone levels are related to preference for the hen. It was established that even completely dark-reared birds come to prefer the stuffed hen over the red box if allowed a period of time in running wheels.[38] Dark-reared birds who were not allowed this period did not develop the preference. It turned out that while exposure to diffuse light was not essential, exposure to patterned light accelerated the emergence of this preference. These results suggest that under conditions likely to be encountered in the chicks' species-typical environment, namely exposure to patterned light and the opportunity to run about, the predisposition will emerge rapidly and strongly. If a chick is raised under laboratory conditions where only one of the necessary conditions from the STE is present, the preference will still emerge. When both necessary conditions from the STE are absent, it will not.

For dark-reared chicks a period of time in running wheels, around 24 hours after hatching, appears to be essential for the hen preference to emerge the following day. In a recent study, Johnson, Davies and Horn[39] investigated the effects on the emergence of the predisposition of allowing dark-reared chicks a period of time in the running wheels at varying ages after hatching. The results indicated that there is a time window between 12 and 36 hours after hatching within which the experience must occur. Time spent in the running wheels before or after these ages does not result in the expression of the predisposition.[40]

The second question relating to the predisposition concerned its specificity or the characteristics of the stuffed hen, which cause it to be preferred over the red box. One possibility is that the stuffed hen is more attractive simply because it has greater outline or textural complexity than the box. There is some evidence that older chicks preferentially approach objects of greater visual complexity,[41] and this preference may also be important in younger chicks. In order to circumvent the problem of quantifying visual complexity,[42] Johnson and Horn[43] compared dark-reared chicks' preference for an intact stuffed hen with their preference for other 'test' objects which were constructed by scrambling or degrading a similar stuffed hen in various ways. In all of the experiments in this series dark-reared chicks were placed in running wheels in darkness 24 hours after hatching. Recall that this procedure had previously been shown to trigger the subsequent emergence of the predisposition: that is, a preference for the stuffed hen over the red box. Twenty-four hours after the time in the wheels (when they were 48 hours old) the chicks were simultaneously presented with an intact stuffed hen and a second test object, and their preference ascertained. If the second object had been the red box we know from the earlier experiments that the chicks would strongly have preferred the hen.

The first 'test' object to which the intact stuffed hen was compared was a stuffed hen which had been partially disarticulated and reassembled in an anatomically unusual way (figure 3.8; top left). With this stimulus there was no significant preference for the intact hen 24 hours after the period in running wheels. This suggested that, while both objects had similarly complex outlines (the same number and shape of wings, legs etc. protuding from the body) and were of similar 'textural' complexity (feather patterns, species markings etc.), the fact that one object had an intact hen outline and the other had jumbled limbs made no difference to their relative attractiveness to the chicks. The next test object investigated was similar to the previous one except that several of the elements (wings, leg, head etc.) were separated from the trunk of the body (figure 3.8; top right). Again, the intact fowl was not significantly preferred over this object, reinforcing the earlier conclusion that an overall hen-shaped outline is not a critical factor for the emerging predisposition: a stuffed hen with a 'scrambled' outline is as attractive as an intact hen. These findings left open several other possibilities including: (a) the chicks possibly responding to a few particular features such as the eyes or beak, or to some specific

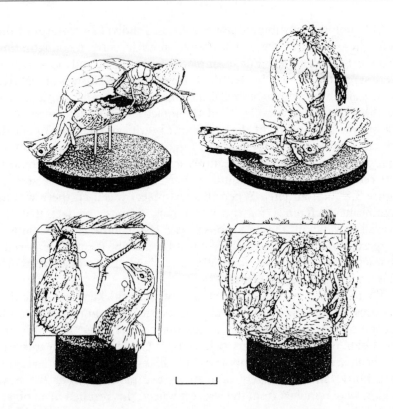

Figure 3.8 *Some of the 'test' objects used in the experiments of Johnson and Horn. Top left: the jumbled stuffed hen; top right: the disarticulated hen; bottom right: the cut-up pelt; bottom left: the 'scrambled' hen. Scale bar = 10 cm. Drawings by Priscilla Barrett.*

arrangements (configuration) of these features, (b) the chicks possibly responding simply to particular feather patterns or colours.

The next test object was composed of the trunk pelt of a hen cut into small squares and jumbled up with other parts of the body, before being stuck onto the cork sides of a rotating box (figure 3.8; bottom right). Using this test object there was a strong preference for the intact hen. For the first time in this series of experiments then, we had a test object that did not contain the essential attractive characteristics. Since the test object possessed the 'textural' complexity and colours of the intact hen these characteristics do not appear to be critical. So, to what particularly were the chicks responding?

Although the cut-up pelt object possessed individual features of the hen, these features were not always in their correct configuration relative to each other. For example, the eye, beak and neck region were separated. It may be that the presence of such clusters of features is critical for the attractiveness of the object. On the other hand, it may be that the greater complexity of the intact fowl outline compared to the simple box outline of the test object is critical. One way to decide which of these two factors is most important is to create a test object that possesses the clusters of features absent in the previous test object, but retains the simple box outline. Such a test object can be seen in figure 3.8 (bottom left). When this test object was used there was no significant preference for the intact hen, despite the fact that the overall outline of the test object was less complex. This finding suggests, therefore, that clusters of features may be the most important characteristic of the hen for the young chick. But which particular clusters of features are critical?

There is some evidence from studies of adult chickens and quail that features of the head and neck are particularly important in the recognition of individuals in a dominance hierarchy[44] and for the elicitation of social proximity behaviour.[45] Could it be that features of the head are particularly important for chicks also? To investigate this possibility, all the clusters of features except those from the head region were removed from the last test object: this resulted in an object that contained the head region only mounted on a rotating box. Much to the surprise of Johnson and Horn, when chicks were allowed to choose between the whole intact hen and the head region alone, there was a tendency for them to prefer the latter! This suggests that not only is the cluster of features associated with the head the critical characteristic to the chick, but that the rest of the hen's body may even act as a 'distractor' from this critical region.

So it seems that the cluster of features of the hen's head are critical. But how specific to the particular species need these features be? To answer this question chicks' preferences for the hen needed to be compared with those toward another species. Initially, another species of fowl, the gadwall duck (*Anas strepera*; see figure 3.9), was chosen. When test chicks were given a choice between these two species they had no preference, suggesting that the critical facial features need not be species specific.[46] Johnson and Horn then enquired whether chicks would also show no preference if tested with the intact hen and a

Figure 3.9 *The stuffed polecat,* Mustela putoris, *and the stuffed gadwall duck,* Anas strepera.

species from a different class. The animal chosen was a polecat (*Mustela putorius*; see figure 3.9). Once again the chicks' behaviour proved surprising; they showed no preference. This finding indicates that the general arrangement of features on the head may be more important than the details of the features themselves.

What then, does all this imply for a chick raised in the natural environment? The specific predisposition just discussed may ensure that the chick attends toward and approaches an appropriate object – normally the chick's own mother, when it emerges from under her on the day after hatching. The young chick then learns about the visual characteristics of the particular adult bird and so comes to recognize her. Since features of the head and neck are particularly important for the predisposition, it may be that this is the region about which the chick learns most. With regard to the STE, the rough specification of the hen's face is all that is needed. Few other things with this specification are found in the young chick's STE.

The Interacting Systems Model of Imprinting

Putting together much of the evidence discussed so far led Horn, Bolhuis and Johnson to propose an *interacting systems* account of imprinting. This account maintains that, in contrast to existing single-process theories of imprinting, there are two dissociable processes underlying filial preference behaviour in the domestic chick. First, a predisposition for the young chick to attend toward visual stimuli, which possess some of the characteristics of a hen and second, a learning system, subserved by IMHV, which can be engaged by a variety of conspicuous objects early in life. In the species-typical environment of the chick it would run about and be exposed to patterned light shortly after hatching. As mentioned earlier, this would ensure that the predisposition would develop strongly and early. The predisposition then would serve to orient the chick preferentially toward adult hens, as opposed to other objects in its visual environment. Following this, the learning system, which could be engaged by many objects that the young chick might attend toward, would learn most about the chick's own mother. Box 3.4 discusses in more detail how the interacting systems model relates to the natural environment of the chick, while box 3.5 describes the case of a particular chick reared in an unnatural environment.

Box 3.4   The interacting systems model and the species-typical environment

When a chick emerges from under the hen it will be exposed to patterned light. It has been demonstrated that exposure to patterned light accelerates the emergence of the preference for hens (Bolhuis *et al.* 1985). Thus, the conditions which a chick encounters shortly after emerging from under its mother, even for brief periods, may ensure the rapid appearance of the specific predisposition. In turn, the presence of the predisposition may ensure that the newly emerged chick will attend toward the head region of the nearest adult bird, normally the mother. Comparatively rapid learning about the characteristics of an individual adult bird's head may be important for at least two reasons. First, association with one female may prevent attacks from others and second, chicks may learn about particular food types by watching or copying what the adult bird pecks (Barthashunas and Suboski, 1984). In other words, the predisposition not only facilitates the chick in learning about mother, but it also helps by getting the chick to pay attention to what mother does, helping it to learn other things.

In most of the laboratory studies we have described, the chicks or ducklings were reared in isolation. However, in the natural situation chicks or ducklings would be reared with siblings. What effect might this social rearing have on the ability to imprint on the hen? In general, rearing chicks with siblings prior to exposure to adult birds depresses but does not eliminate imprinting on the hen (Guiton, 1959; Zajonc *et al.*, 1975). Rearing ducklings with siblings during the period of exposure to a stuffed mallard hen also interferes with maternal imprinting (Lickliter and Gottlieb, 1986a). However, social interaction with own species brood mates after a period of filial imprinting may strengthen or maintain subsequent preference for the mother (Lickliter and Gottlieb, 1986b, 1988). As yet, little is known about the role of siblings in imprinting on a live hen in the natural situation.

Several predictions arise from the interacting systems account:

1 If the two systems are truly dissociable then damaging IMHV will affect the chick's ability to learn, but will not affect the predisposition. This prediction has been confirmed: chicks with small lesions to IMHV respond like dark-reared birds in preference tests even if

they have previously been exposed to an imprinting object like the red box.[47]

2 Chicks should be capable of learning to discriminate between individual adult chickens. In order to test this hypothesis, two-day-old chicks were exposed to one of two individually different stuffed hens for about four hours (see figure 3.10). Two hours after the end of training the birds were given a choice test between the two stuffed hens. In accordance with prediction, chicks were significantly more likely to start to approach the particular individual hen which they had seen previously.[48]

3 Damage to IMHV should prevent the chick from being able to learn about individual adult birds. In order to test this hypothesis, chicks

Box 3.5   The story of Egbert

With reference to imprinting in the species-typical environment, we report an anecdotal account of the fatal consequences of a chick hatching out in an abnormal environment*.

During British army tank manoeuvres in the Middle East in 1945 the tank crews would often exchange portions of their rations for local eggs. Unfortunately, due to the heat some of the eggs were not as fresh as they might have been and little Egbert, a black chick, hatched out into a frying pan in the middle of the Syrian desert. The tank crew were only too pleased to acquire a fluffy mascot and fed Egbert on crushed army biscuits. Thus, Egbert became the latest in a long line of soliders' pets that had included tortoises, chameleons and Syrian ground spiders. After a few days the tank crew noticed that Egbert would follow army boots. Whenever someone walked past, Egbert would scurry after them attempting to nestle up to the boots. For fear of treading on Egbert in the confined space inside the tank, the men built a small carrying case out of packaging. After travelling several hundred miles in the tank, the crew arrived at a central rendezvous and set up camp. Egbert spent some happy days following army boots through the tent guy ropes until one day he snuggled up to the corporal's size nine boots during parade. When the order to 'stand to attention' was barked out Egbert met a sad end, a victim of being raised outside his species-typical environment.

* We are indebted to Mr D. Dixon of Weymouth for the story.

Figure 3.10 *The two stuffed hens (jungle fowl) used as training stimuli in the Johnson and Horn study. Half of the chicks were trained on one and half on the other. Scale bar = 10 cm. Drawings by Priscilla Barrett.*

with small bilateral IMHV lesions and chicks with similar small lesions to a different part of the forebrain were exposed to individual stuffed hens before being given a choice test as described above. Chicks with the control lesions, like intact chicks, preferred the particular individual hen to which they had previously been exposed. In contrast, chicks with IMHV lesions had no preference.[49] Thus, chicks without a functioning IMHV are not able to learn about the characteristics of an individual hen, although they do show the *primal* preference for hens in general.

4 It should be easier to reverse preferences acquired through exposure to artificial stimuli than to reverse preferences acquired through exposure to a hen (or other similar object). This is because during the reversal phase of the experiment both the predisposition and the learning process contribute to preference (see box 3.6 for details). In a series of experiments Bolhuis and Trooster[50] established that there is a strong asymmetry in the ease of reversibility between these two stimuli in the predicted direction: birds initially trained on the hen did not change their preferences following exposure to the red box. Birds initially trained on the red box did shift their preference following exposure to the hen.

Box 3.6   The reversibility of acquired preferences

There is ample evidence to show that a preference for an artificial object can be reversed following prolonged exposure to a second object (see for example, Salzen and Meyer, 1967). However, the results of recent experiments indicate that information about the first imprinting object to which a chick is exposed is not forgotten and that, under certain circumstances, the original preference may return or 'resurface'. For instance, Cherfas and Scott (1981) exposed domestic chicks to a coloured ball for a period of three days, which resulted in a strong preference for this object compared to a ball of a different colour. When the original stimulus was removed and the chicks were exposed to a ball of a different colour for a similar period, there was a significant change in preference score toward the latter. However, when both objects were removed from the chicks' home cage for a further period of three days, Cherfas and Scott reported a significant change in preference back toward the first object.

Bolhuis and Trooster (1988) at the University of Groningen exposed day-old chicks to either a stuffed hen or a red box for two hours. The chicks in both groups showed a strong preference for the training stimulus in a subsequent preference test involving the two objects. The next day the chicks were exposed to the alternative object for two hours, and preferences were tested again. There was a reversal of preference score in the group initially exposed to the box (box–hen group), but no significant change in preference score in the group of chicks that had been exposed to the stuffed hen first (hen–box group). This result was obtained even in an experiment in which the relative attractiveness of the two objects had been manipulated such that the chicks initially trained on the box had a significantly greater preference score than the chicks trained on the stuffed fowl. Bolhuis and Trooster argued that, in the box–hen situation, the emerging predisposition and the effects of exposure to the second object would affect the chicks' preferences in the same direction in the second phase of the experiment, resulting in a preference for the hen. When the chicks were first exposed to the stuffed hen, the two systems were in conflict in the second phase of the experiment, resulting in a relatively stable preference for the hen. We illustrate this in figure 3.7. The two ovals correspond to the two systems which influence preference, the one on the left being the learning mechanism, and the one on the right being the *primal* hen preference. Between T1 and T2 the *primal* preference for the hen has emerged. It is clear that the group initially trained on the box will reverse their overall preference more readily than will the group of chicks trained on the hen first.

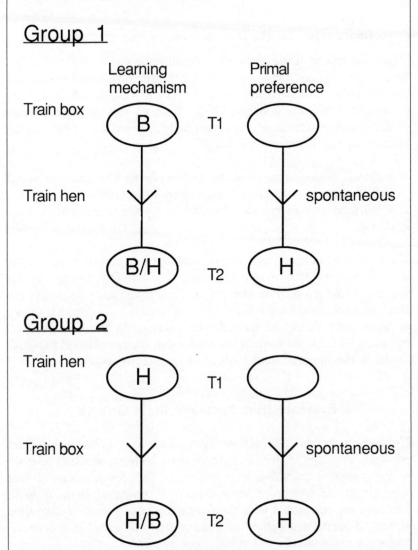

Figure 3.11 *An account of the Bolhuis and Trooster experiment. For each group there are two preference systems: a learning system (left) and a primal preference system (right).*

In conclusion, the evidence obtained so far is generally consistent with the predictions of the interacting systems account of imprinting.

Implications for the Development of Face Recognition

This brief review of the ethological literature on species and individual face recognition and the extent to which they involve *primal* structures, has led us to consider one species in which these issues have been studied in detail, the domestic chick. We then reported that current evidence supports the contention that there are two dissociable systems underlying this behaviour in chicks:

1 A *primal* device underlying the preference for the chick to orient toward clusters of features possessed by conspecifics.
2 A learning system engaged by objects to which the young chick attends.

We argued in chapter two that the apparent U-shaped curve in the development of face recognition over the first few months of life suggested that more than one process was involved. Obviously, the chick and the infant are widely differing species, and parallels drawn between then should be treated with caution. In the next chapter, however, we hope to convince the reader that the extension of the chick model to the human infant leads to some exciting insights.

Evidence from Postnatal Brain Growth

Up to now in this chapter we have discussed the evidence from ethology. Another source of evidence from biology, which is relevant to generating a cognitive level theory of the development of face recognition, derives from some aspects of postnatal brain growth. Since we are concerned with the development of a visual recognition ability, it seems reasonable to assume that the state of the neural pathways that underlie this process are critical.

There are two main visual pathways in humans: the 'geniculostriate' pathway and the 'retinotectal' pathway. Figure 3.12 shows a grossly simplified drawing of the two visual pathways discussed. The 'geniculostriate' pathway passes from the retina to the primary visual cortex via the lateral geniculate nucleus (LGN). Although this pathway

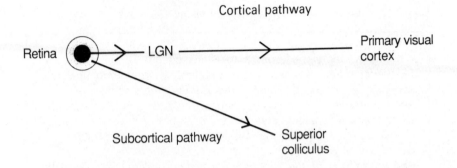

Figure 3.12 *A schematic representation of the two main visual pathways in humans.*

involves some subcortical structures such as the LGN, for convenience we will refer to it as the *cortical* pathway. The retinotectal pathway passes from the retina to a subcortical structure, the superior colliculus. We will refer to this pathway as the *subcortical* pathway, although it is worth noting that this pathway involves some cortical projections. In most mammals the cortical pathway receives input largely from retinal cells in the fovea, while the subcortical pathway receives input primarily from cells in the peripheral parts of the retina.[51] Some authors have characterized the functional distinction between the two pathways as the subcortical pathway being primarily involved in computing the spatial location of a stimulus, whereas the cortical pathway is involved in processing the details of the visual characteristics of a stimulus: the 'where' and the 'what' pathways. This characterization of functions is, however, certainly over-simplified.

In 1974, Gordon Bronson proposed that the primary visual pathway does not gain control over sensory motor behaviour in the human infant until around the second or third month of life.[52] The evidence in support of this contention came from a variety of different sources and is reviewed in box 3.7. Over the first month or so of life then, Bronson and others[53] believe that the infant is responding to visual stimuli primarily by means of the subcortical visual pathway.

Box 3.7   The postnatal development of visual pathways

Although a variety of different criteria have been used as indicators of functional maturation, no single criterion has met with universal acceptance. For this reason it is important both to discuss a range of neuroanatomical and neurophysiological 'markers' of maturation, and to compare the relative state of development of several pathways (These points are discussed in more detail in Johnson, 1990b.)

The maturation of the subcortical visual pathway. The subcortical visual pathway in the human begins to myelinate about two months prenatally and the process is completed about three months after birth. This is in contrast to the cortical pathway where the process of myelinization begins only at about the time of birth (Yakovlev and Lecours, 1967).

Very little anatomical information is available with regard to the structural development of the human retina due to its great delicacy and the difficulty in obtaining samples. However, a recent study of the retinal morphology of an eight-day-old infant (Abramov *et al.*, 1982), confirmed the earlier suggestion (Mann, 1964) that while the peripheral retina is relatively mature at birth, the foveal region is still very immature. This observation led Abramov and his colleagues to suggest that neonatal visual acuity is mainly due to extrafoveal vision. Myelinization of the optic nerve proceeds rapidly in the first four months of life, thereafter progressing less rapidly to reach adult levels at about two years of age (Freide and Hu, 1967). By 24 weeks of gestation the adult pattern of lamination in the superior colliculus can be observed (Stampalija and Kostovic, 1981).

The maturation of the cortical visual pathway. In the human the lateral geniculate nucleus doubles in total volume between birth and six months (Huttenlocher *et al.*, 1982). Although most cell types can be recognized at birth (de Courten and Garey, 1982), they differ from their mature forms by possessing many more spiny processes on the dendritic shafts and soma. Hairs and spines reach a maximum at about four months after birth, before reducing to adult numbers by nine months. During this time the cell body size increases although the total dendritic length decreases due to the more complex branching pattern at birth (Leuba and Garey, 1982).

The characteristic pattern of an increase in dendritic arborization followed by a subsequent decline appears to be true of at least some neurones in the human primary visual cortex. Spines become more numerous in the weeks following birth reaching a peak at about four or five months of age (Leuba and Garey, 1987). A parallel rise is found in the density of synapses which reaches a peak at eight months postnatal (Huttenlocher *et al.*, 1982). At birth many cells are in inappropriate layers, and fibres are poorly myelinated (Conel, 1939–67). Myelination of intracortical neurones appears to continue into mid-childhood.

Evoked potentials evidence. Many studies have been undertaken on visually evoked potentials (VEP) in young infants (see Atkinson, 1984 for a review). In general, they show that components of the VEP thought to be related to the subcortex are present from birth, and some components related to the striate cortex are present from around the time of birth. More specific components of cortical origin (fast high-frequency wavelets), however, do not appear in infants under four weeks (Schanel-Klitsch and Siegfried, 1987). Further, VEP responses to changes in the orientation of moving bars are not manifest until six weeks of age (Braddick, *et al.*, 1986). The evoked potentials evidence thus gives general credence to the idea that cortical functioning develops over the first few months, and that some major changes occur in the second month of life. However, the evidence is also indicative of some cortical activity at birth.

Beyond the Subcortical to Cortical Shift

In recent years the notion of a shift from subcortical to cortical visual processing in early infancy has come under criticism for several reasons. First, there has been increasing evidence for apparently sophisticated perceptual abilities in the first few weeks of life.[54] For example, since it is believed by some that the processing abilities of the subcortical visual pathway is relatively crude, the new-born's ability to perceive 3-dimensional information is often taken as evidence of cortical visual pathway functioning. Second, recent knowledge about cortical visual processing has brought into question the notion of one cortical visual pathway. Recent evidence suggests that two or more distinct cortical pathways should be considered.[55] These considerations have led several authors to propose some form of partial cortical functioning at birth.[56] As yet, however, the nature of this partial cortical functioning remains poorly specified.

One of us (Johnson) has recently proposed a hypothesis regarding the development of visual attention and its relation to cortical maturation.[57] This hypothesis specifies the extent of cortical functioning in the new-born, and accounts for changes in the development of overt visual attention over the first few months of life in terms of the maturation of three separate cortical pathways. These three pathways and a fourth, subcortical pathway, are based on proposals put forward to account for adult primate electrophysiological and lesion data by Peter Schiller from Massachusetts Institute of Technology (see figure 3.13).[58] The four pathways are:

1 A pathway from the retina to the superior colliculus thought to be involved in the generation of eye movements toward simple, easily discriminable stimuli, and fed mainly by the peripheral visual field. This pathway corresponds to the *subcortical* pathway discussed earlier.
2 A cortical pathway that goes to the superior colliculus from the

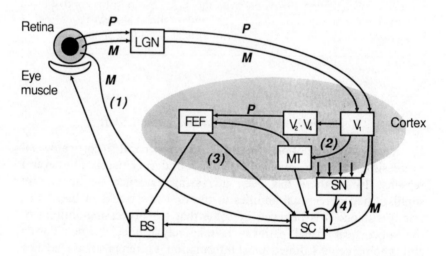

Figure 3.13   *A schematic representation of the model proposed by Schiller for the neuroanatomical pathways thought to underlie oculomotor control in primates. LGN = lateral geniculate nucleus; SC = superior colliculus; MT = medial temporal area; BS = brain stem; FEF = frontal eye fields; M = broad band (magnocellular) stream; P = colour opponent (parvocellular) stream; V_1 = primary visual cortex; $V_2 - V_4$ = other visual cortical areas; SN = substantia nigra – inhibitory connections from cortex. Adapted from Johnson (1990a).*

primary visual cortex and also via the middle temporal area (MT), the *MT* pathway.

3 A cortical pathway where both broad-band and colour-opponent streams of processing converge to the frontal eye fields (FEF), the *FEF* pathway, which is involved in the detailed and complex analysis of visual stimuli and the temporal sequencing of eye movements within complex arrays.

4 An inhibitory input to the colliculus from several cortical areas via the substantia nigra and basal ganglia, the *inhibitory* pathway. The function of this pathway may be to prevent the colliculus from initiating a saccade toward a target appearing in the peripheral visual field.

Two proposals have been put forward by Johnson with regard to these pathways and their correspondence to the development of visually guided behaviour in the infant. First, that the characteristics of visually guided behaviour in the infant at particular ages is determined by which of these pathways is functional, and second, which of these pathways is functional is constrained, in turn, by the maturational state of the primary visual cortex.

We will discuss the second of these proposals first. The primate cortex is a six-layered structure with each layer possessing particular neuron types and patterns of interconnectivity. Input and output connections to any area of cortex to or from other areas of the brain also arrive and depart from particular layers. This layer-wise pattern of inputs and outputs becomes particularly important when we consider the postnatal development of the cortex. This is because, by several neuroanatomical measures, the human cortex develops postnatally from the deeper layers toward those closest to the surface of the brain.[59] This 'inside-out' layer-wise pattern of postnatal maturation has particular consequences for the outputs from the primary visual cortex, since the three cortical pathways mentioned earlier all pass through the region and depart from different layers. It should be clear, therefore, that the sequence of development of the outputs to the three cortical pathways can be predicted from knowledge of postnatal growth in the primary visual pathway, the essential 'gateway' for information from the retina. Employing this basic logic Johnson proposed several stages of the development of visually guided behaviour, with each transition being caused by the 'enabling' of one or other of the three cortical pathways initially discussed by Schiller.

The new-born

The 'inside-out' layer-wise pattern of cortical development means that in the new-born infant only the deeper layers of the primary visual cortex are capable of performing computations on visual input. Since the outputs to the FEF and MT pathways depart from the middle and upper layers, these pathways are assumed not to be processing information at the time of birth. However, as described in box 3.7, evidence from visually evoked potentials suggests that information is entering the primary visual cortex. Furthermore, a pathway that departs from the deepest layer of the primary visual cortex will influence the activity of the subcortical pathway. Thus, while Gordon Bronson was right to claim that most of the new-born's visual behaviour can be accounted for in terms of processing in the subcortical pathway, there is also some reason to believe that information processing occurs in the deeper layers of the primary visual cortex at birth. The circuits present in the new-born are illustrated in figure 3.14 (a).

One month of age

Due to the continuing maturation of the primary visual cortex upward from the deeper layers, over the first few weeks of life the output to the inhibitory pathway (4) becomes functional. As mentioned earlier, this pathway is involved in supressing the response of the colliculus to new stimuli impinging on the peripheral visual field. As a consequence, the infant will no longer respond as readily to stimuli presented within its visual field. This behavioural phenomenon, often known as 'obligatory attention' is reported to be particularly prevalent in infants around one month of age. Such infants will appear to 'lock on' to a particular stimulus for as long as several minutes. Distracting stimuli placed to one or other side of the stimulus have little or no effect on the direction of gaze. Figure 3.14 (b) illustrates the neural circuits proposed to underlie visually guided behaviour in infants around one month of age.

Two months of age

Further maturation of the primary visual cortex results in an output from the middle layers to the MT pathway. This pathway has been associated with the ability of primates to track a moving object

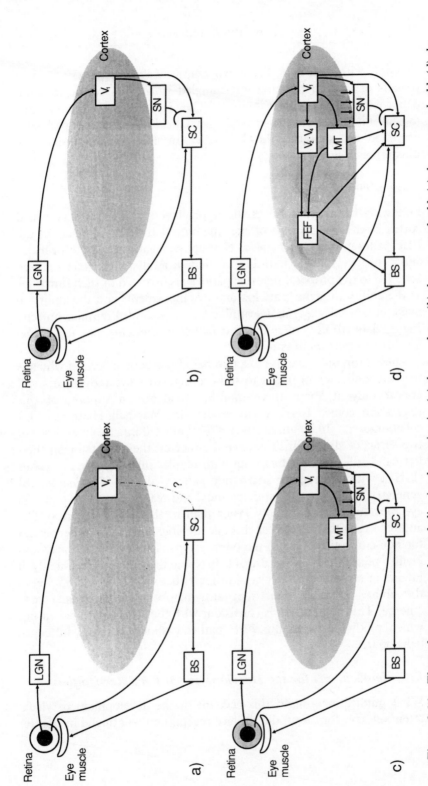

Figure 3.14 *The pathways proposed to underlie visual attention in: (a) the new-born; (b) the one-month-old; (c) the two-month-old; (d) the three-month-old. See Figure 3.13 for explanation of symbols.*

smoothly with their eyes. From two months of age infants start to show periods of smooth tracking intermingled with the saccadic tracking patterns found in younger infants.[60] They also become more sensitive to stimuli placed in the central visual field. The neural pathways proposed to subserve the behaviour of the two-month-old are illustrated in figure 3.14 (c).

Three months and older

Following the maturation of the upper layers of the primary visual cortex after three months of age, the output from these layers to the FEF pathway becomes enabled. Neurophysiological studies in primates and neuropsychological studies on human adults with brain damage have led to the proposal that this pathway is involved in such functions as the ability to make 'anticipatory' eye movements and the ability to make organized sequential scanning patterns toward familiar objects. Figure 3.14 (d) illustrates the four pathways thought to be functional by three to four months of age.

These proposals give rise to a number of predictions, one of which is that the ability of an infant to show anticipatory eye movements will appear only at about three months. Evidence in support of this suggestion comes from recent studies by Marshall Haith and his collaborators.[61] In an initial study 3.5-month-old infants viewed one of two series of slides which appeared either on their right- or on their left-hand side, either alternating with regular inter-stimulus intervals (ISI) or with an irregular alternation pattern and ISI. The regular ISI generated more stimulus anticipations, and reaction times to make an eye movement were reliably faster than in the irregular series. The authors argue that infants of this age are able to develop expectancies for non-controllable spatio-temporal events. Robinson, McCarty and Haith[62] report that they were unable to obtain these effects consistently in infants of six and nine weeks old. Thus, between nine and 15 weeks the ability to make consistent anticipatory eye movements may emerge. This observation is consistent with the theory outlined earlier which predicted when the FEF pathway should start to influence behaviour.

Implications for the Development of Face Recognition

What implications might this account of the development of visual attention have for the studies of face recognition mentioned in chapter two? Let us start with the new-born. Characteristics of the functioning of the subcortical visual pathway are taken to include that it is involved in the generation of saccades toward simple, easily discriminable stimuli that appear in the peripheral visual field. Johnson, following Bronson, accounts for some aspects of the new-born's visuo-motor behaviour in terms of the functioning of such a system. Figure 3.15, for example, shows a schematic representation of the eye movements of a very young infant as it attempts to track a slowly moving object.

Notice two things about this tracking behaviour in comparison to that of an older infant (also figure 3.15). First, the tracking is *pursuit*, i.e., it lags behind the movement of the stimulus. Second, it is *saccadic*, i.e., it is a series of 'steps' rather than a smooth eye movement. These two characteristics would be expected if the mechanism underlying this behaviour were only responding to a stimulus once it moved out of foveal vision. One reason for this is that, at birth, the fovea is still very immature while the peripheral retina is comparatively well developed (see box 3.7). Thus, the output to the

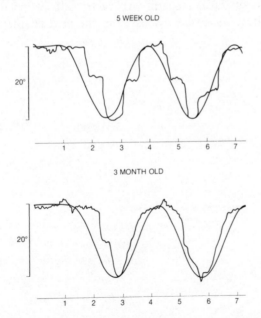

Figure 3.15   *Visual following of moving targets by two infants. The smooth lines indicate the movement of the target; the jagged lines indicate the movement of the eyes. The scale is in seconds. Younger infants are incapable of tracking smoothly (after Aslin, 1981).*

mechanism that controls tracking need only be extra-foveal. When the moving stimulus activates extra-foveal cells it 'triggers' a saccade which re-foveates the stimulus. Recall, also, that any extra-foveal input projects primarily to the subcortical visual pathway. Thus, we reach the initially surprising conclusion that new-born tracking may be largely subcortically mediated. Other characteristic aspects of the new-born infant's visuo-motor behaviour can be accounted for by means of the same mechanism.[63]

We said earlier that the foveal retinal cells mainly fed the cortical visual pathways, and that the MT pathway became functional at around two months of age. We explained in chapter two how in the infant-control testing procedure the infant looks toward a single static stimulus presented straight ahead. Thus, it is possible that the infant-control testing procedure is a good 'marker' for cortical functioning, in the same way that saccadic tracking may be a good 'marker' for subcortical visuo-spatial processing. Is it possible, therefore, that in the human infant there are two dissociable systems underlying the development of face recognition, each with a particular neural circuitry? These issues are discussed in the next chapter.

4

Conspec, Conlern and the Development of Face Recognition

From our discussion so far we can draw three conclusions;

1 *Existing accounts of the development of face recognition are inadequate in that they posit only one mechanism underlying this process.* In chapter two we reported that we were able to replicate *both* the finding that one-month old infants show no face preference *and* the finding that newborn infants prefer faces. We have, therefore, what looks like a developmental U-shaped curve, something not easily accounted for in terms of the development of a single underlying mechanism.

2 *Evidence from other species supports a two-system account of the ability to recognize other members of the species.* In chapter three we described how, in the chick, there is strong evidence to support a two-system account of the development of conspecific recognition. The first of the two systems did not require exposure to a conspecific, but caused the young animal to attend more to objects resembling conspecifics. Within the species-typical environment, this would lead the chick to attend toward its mother. It was suggested that this first system serves to bias the input to the second system, which learned by exposure to objects that the young chick attended toward. The two systems were demonstrated to have dissociable neural substrates.

3 *In the human infant there is a general shift from subcortical to cortical visual processing over the first few months of life.* Also in chapter three we reviewed evidence in support of the contention that there is a general shift from subcortical to cortical processing over the

first few months of life. When put together with other information, we suggested that the *infant-control task*, where single stimuli are presented directly in front of the infant, can be characterized as being mediated by the cortical pathway, whereas performance in the *tracking task*, where infants re-orient toward stimuli outside the foveal field, can be viewed as indicative of functioning in the subcortical pathway.

In this chapter we use the information gleaned from biology to develop a multi-system theory of the development of face recognition in the human infant.

We will begin by discussing the nature of the ability of new-borns to recognize a face. The debate on this topic can be characterized by two extreme positions: *sensory* and *structural*. The *sensory* hypothesis holds that facilitation of face identification results from non-specific characteristics of the infant sensory system. The opposing view would be that specific *structural* information about the general characteristics of faces is present without prior exposure to these objects. Major proponents of the sensory hypothesis of new-born face recognition are Kathleen Kleiner, now at the University of Indiana, and Martin Banks at the University of California, Berkeley. They described the structural hypothesis as thus: 'young infants are predisposed to attend to social stimuli'. Their definition of the sensory hypothesis was that 'infants are predisposed to attend to stimuli that are readily visible . . . [F]acelike patterns are fixated preferentially because they contain large [low spatial frequency], high contrast features that are arranged symmetrically'.[1] Notice, however, that these two viewpoints are at opposite ends of a continuum, and that various intermediate positions are possible. For example, the structural hypothesis could be couched in terms of the multi-dimensional visual characteristics of faces.

New-born Abilities

Evidence in Support of the Sensory Hypothesis

The fundamental assumption of the sensory hypotheses is that certain classes of stimuli are preferred by young infants solely as a result of the general properties of the early stages of sensory processing. That is, the preferences of new-borns are attributable to lower order characteristics of stimuli. For example, suppose we are able to establish that, irrespective of the size, young infants prefer round objects over any other shape. Suppose further that we establish that they prefer dark red things over any other colour regardless of shape or size. It is clear that such an infant would prefer cherries over most other foodstuffs, but we would not want to claim that there was a *primal* mechanism underlying a preference for cherries *per se*. Cherries just happen to be a thing that satisfies a couple of unidimensional sensory preferences.

In the various theories of infant visual preference which have been proposed, experiments have often been carried out with stimuli other than faces. Such experiments estimate the infants' 'interest' in a stimulus by measuring the amount of time they look at it when first presented with it. Alternatively, pairs of stimuli are presented to the infants, and the amount of time spent looking at each is compared. By such methods, certain stimulus properties have been identified as influencing the infants' gaze. By this view, faces may not be a special class of stimulus, but may merely be preferred in certain situations by virtue of the pattern possessing certain psychophysical properties.[2]

What psychophysical properties affect infants' preferences for visual stimuli? A large number of stimulus variables have been proposed including contour density, size, kind of motion, distance, brightness, complexity, contrast, colour, size and number of elements and spatial frequency characteristics. For example, Karmel[3] suggested that the amount of contour in a stimulus – 'the sum of all the lengths of black–white transition [is a] major influence' on preference. This theory was not aimed at accounting for the infants' preference for faces. However, more recent theories, and in particular the proponents of the *linear systems model* (LSM), have explicitly made the claim that faces are no different from other visual stimuli. They are preferred simply because they happen to have appropriate stimulus properties – rather like the cherries in the example discussed earlier.

For the first few months of life, infants' preferences for patterns other than faces are well predicted by the linear systems model.[4] This model, a form of the sensory hypothesis, predicts infants' preferences on the basis of a particular kind of analysis of the stimuli, the Fourier transform. Basically, the model claims that infant preferences for visual patterns are determined solely by their visibility to the infant (see box 4.1). The linear systems model is particularly good at predicting infants' preferences with high-contrast patterns such as regular checks,[5] rectangular gratings,[6] bull's-eyes[7] and patterns of

Box 4.1 The Linear Systems Model

It is by now common knowledge that any complex sound is made up of components of a range of frequencies. The tone controls on our radios or hi-fi serve to selectively amplify either the high or the low frequency parts of the voice or musical instrument we happen to be listening to, irrespective of the pitch. Although it might seem counter-intuitive, visual patterns can be split up in a similar way, but now we must think in terms of two dimensions rather than one. For any visual pattern, two functions may be derived: the amplitude spectrum, comprising the amplitude and orientation of the component spatial frequencies, and the phase spectrum, comprised of the phases and orientations of the components. The amplitude spectrum shows us how much energy there is at different frequencies and the phase spectrum, roughly speaking, shows us how that energy is arranged. The phase spectrum, then, indicates the form of the image.

The linear systems model holds that the attractiveness of patterns in early infancy is determined solely by the amount of effective energy in the patterns. This means that only the amplitude spectrum will be useful in predicting the attractiveness of a particular pattern. Phase information will not be of any relevance. The relationship between the amplitude spectrum of a pattern and the effective energy depends on who is looking at the patterns. The visual systems of new-born infants, starting at the retina, are relatively ill formed and filter the pattern being fixated, particularly at high frequencies. The infant's sensitivity to energy at different frequencies can be determined by using simple stimuli (rather like determining an audiogram for one's hearing). This produces the contrast sensitivity function (CSF). The attractiveness of any pattern, then, can be estimated by summing the amplitude spectrum over all orientations and filtering it through the CSF.

The new-born's visual system is most sensitive to frequencies between 0.2 and 0.5 cycles/degree (Atkinson and Braddick, 1981; Atkinson, Braddick and French, 1979). The stimulus with most energy in that region would be a check pattern with check size of about half an inch seen from about a one-foot distance.

stripes.[8] Variations on the model also predict infant preference with irregular checks of different sizes.[9] It does not necessarily follow, however, that it will predict infant preferences for stimuli of other kinds, for example those without sharp contours, or with low contrast or irregular curves. Whether or not preferences with such stimuli can be predicted by the LSM remains an empirical issue. But, by this theory, the explanation for young infants' preference for faces over other stimuli would be ascribed simply to the greater visibility of faces.

Evidence in Support of the Structural Hypothesis

The alternative to the sensory hypothesis holds that the neonate brain contains *primal* information concerning the structure of faces. That is, the *primal* information is at a higher level than that proposed by versions of the sensory hypothesis. To consider the cherry example again, the structural hypothesis states that cherries are preferred because of the specific combination of features (being red *and* round). Parsimony dictates that we need to rule out lower level sensory hypotheses before we embrace any such structural hypotheses. It would also be unwise, however, to rule out a structural hypothesis a priori. In this section we consider evidence in support of the structural hypothesis. In order to explore this position, however, we need to define more clearly what a structural hypothesis regarding face recognition would look like. We will do this by proposing the term 'Conspec' to refer to a cognitive mechanism in the neonate's brain with the following properties:

1 The mechanism contains structural information concerning the visual characteristics possessed by conspecifics. By 'structural', we mean that the information is concerned with relative spatial location of elements within a pattern and is not decomposable into component phase or amplitude spectra. Such a specification might be as coarsely defined as three high-contrast blobs in the correct relative locations for two eyes and a mouth. The information contained within Conspec need only be sufficient to select the parents' faces from the set of likely stimuli in the species-typical environment. It need not be species or even class specific. We nevertheless use the term Conspec for the device, since it specifies conspecifics *in the context of the species-typical environment.*

2 Conspec information is available without the organism having to be exposed to specific stimuli. The device may, however, require non-specific stimulation to 'trigger' or to 'validate'[10] its functioning.

Note that there are a number of options with regard to how a Conspec may operate and interact with other cognitive mechanisms. For example, a Conspec might regulate approach behaviour, or it could control the allocation of attention.

Conspec and the Chick

As discussed earlier (p. 64), it has been proposed that there are two dissociable neural systems underlying filial preference behaviour in the domestic chick. Does the system underlying the predisposition meet any or all of the requirements just mentioned for a Conspec?

The first requirement for our definition of Conspec concerns the presence within the device of structural information. As discussed in chapter three, a series of experiments with the chick have demonstrated that the specific predisposition is not exclusively due to any simple parameters of the stimulus such as colour, outline complexity or textural richness. Instead, features of the head and neck of the adult hen in their correct arrangement appear to be critical for expression of the preference. However, the features of the head and neck do not have to be specific to the chick's own species. We know this because the head and neck region of other species of a similar size were just as effective (see p. 62).

The second requirement we stipulated for Conspec is that the preference device should operate in a specific manner without specific prior experience. As reported in chapter three, it has been established that chicks do not require any visual experience for expression of the predisposition, but that the preference will emerge following a period of motor activity. This period of motor activity must occur between 12 and 36 hours after hatching.[11] One possibility is that this activity leads to an increase in the level of the hormone testosterone which, in turn, leads to the facilitation of neural circuits underlying Conspec.[12] We now explore the proposal that the human infant, as well as the chick, possess such a Conspec mechanism.

Conspec and the Human New-born

Structural information

Before we can consider the possibility of the new-born infant possessing some structural information about faces, we must thoroughly examine the extent to which face preferences can be accounted for by sensory hypotheses. In other words, can the apparent preference shown by new-born infants for face-like stimuli over scrambled faces, which we discussed in chapter two, be accounted for entirely by the amplitude spectrum of the stimuli (as would be predicted by the linear systems model)?

Neither the Goren *et al.* experiment with new-borns nor the replication by Dziurawiec and Ellis, discussed in chapter two, had the necessary control stimuli to address this issue. One experiment on face preferences which has manipulated amplitude and phase spectra appropriately, however, is that performed by Kathleen Kleiner.[13] Kleiner used a preference paradigm with 48 infants of an average age of 1.7 days. In her experiment, the basic stimuli were a schematic face and a lattice pattern. These stimuli were subjected to a computer analysis into the component amplitude and phase spectra, which were then recombined to create two new 'crossed' stimuli, one created from the amplitude spectrum of the face together with the phase spectrum of a lattice pattern (Af-Pl), and another created from the amplitude spectrum of the lattice together with the phase spectrum of the face (Al-Pf). The stimuli are shown in figure 4.1. The prediction of the linear systems model, described in box 4.1, is that new-borns' preferences would depend entirely on amplitude spectrum and not at all on the phase spectrum. In Kleiner's experiment, the role of phase information was tested by presenting the lattice (Al-Pl), together with the crossed stimulus with the amplitude of the lattice but the phase of the face (Al-Pf). The new-born infants showed no preference between these stimuli. The phase spectrum of the face, therefore, had no influence on preference.

Kleiner and Banks put forward the specific hypothesis that the amplitude spectrum of the face was optimal for the new-born. It would follow, then, that any stimulus with the spectrum of the face would be preferred to any stimulus with the amplitude spectrum of the lattice. This prediction turned to be correct for all four of the appropriate comparisons, including, most surprisingly, the comparison where the

Figure 4.1 *Reproductions of the stimuli used in the experiments of Kleiner (1987); Kleiner and Banks (1987). We refer to the stimuli in terms of the amplitude, 'A', and phase, 'P', spectra. The face stimulus, Af–Pf, has the amplitude spectrum and the phase spectrum of the face. The lattice stimulus, Al–Pl, has the amplitude spectrum and the phase spectrum of the lattice. The crossed stimulus, Al–Pf, has the amplitude spectrum of the lattice and the phase spectrum of the face. The crossed stimulus, Af–Pl, has the amplitude spectrum of the face and the phase spectrum of the lattice. From Kleiner (1987).*

crossed stimulus with the amplitude spectrum of the face (Af-Pl) was preferred to the crossed stimulus with the amplitude spectrum of the lattice (Al-Pf). However, Kleiner's data produced one crucial result which is not predicted by the linear systems model. As already stated, the model explicitly claims that phase information would be irrelevant to new-borns' preferences. To the new-born, then, the crossed stimulus with the amplitude spectrum of the face (Af-Pl) should be just as attractive as the schematic face (Af-Pf). Note that this is a critical prediction for the LSM as it applies to faces.

With these two critical stimuli differing only in phase information, the new-borns overwhelmingly preferred the face. This preference was, in fact, one of the strongest found in the entire experiment. We conclude therefore, from Kleiner's data, that very shortly after birth the human new-born possesses structural information about faces.[14] That is, new-borns possess some specification of the features of a face together with their relative location in space.

Is exposure to faces required?

Before we can conclude that the human new-born possess a *primal* mechanism containing structural information about faces, we also need to demonstrate that this information is unlikely to have been learned. Obviously, we cannot apply the rearing techniques used with chicks to address this issue. Instead, we have to consider indirect evidence and then assess the balance of likelihood. The infants in the original Goren *et al.* experiment were, on average, nine minutes old. In the replication of this study in Aberdeen the mean age at testing was around 40 minutes after birth. While we cannot entirely rule out the possibility of very rapid learning, there are least two sources of indirect evidence which suggest that the information about faces may be *primal*.

The first point is that if learning is taking place over the first few minutes and hours of life, then we would expect to find a positive correlation between age and some measure of face preference. In the Dziurawiec and Ellis study, and in our own new-born studies (to be discussed in chapter five), there is no such positive correlation between postnatal age and the extent to which the face is preferred. With large samples of infants, and a range of ages from 20 to 126 minutes, we have found only small (not significant) negative correlations. When we include infants tested on the second day of life, up to 2,000 minutes, there is still no hint of a positive correlation. This strong evidence against learning is supported by anecdotal observations of infants over the first days of life which suggest that the total time spent looking at faces over this period may amount to only a few minutes at most.[15]

The second source of evidence comes from studies on the phenomenon of neonatal imitation of lip movements, which occurs in the first week of life. This has recently been demonstrated with infants only a minute or two after birth, and under conditions where the model face is the first face seen after birth.[16] While the relationship between imitation and face preference is unclear, it would seem plausible that their emergence should be subject to similar constraints.

Learning about Faces

Earlier in this chapter we defined the characteristics of a *primal* mechanism, Conspec. In the preceding section we confirmed that the human infant showed evidence of possessing such a device which effectively provides the new-born with information concerning the visual characteristics of biologically relevant objects. At the moment, we do not have enough data to say whether the human Conspec is sufficiently detailed to allow unique identification of the human face but, by analogy with the chick, there is no reason to expect it to be so specific. In chapter five we will discuss this question further. Regardless of this, however, the human infant will also need to learn the visual characteristics of a number of individuals. Initially, the infant may only recognize its mother, but soon enough differences among many other individuals will be acquired.

We now wish to consider some of the properties of the system by which the young of any species learn to identify particular faces of members of their species. We propose the term 'Conlern' to describe the variety of systems that might serve this function. Conlern *is a device that acquires and retains specific information about the visual characteristics of individual conspecifics.* There are a number of questions concerning a Conlern. The first set of issues concern the relationship between the mechanisms and representations underlying Conspec and those underlying either Conlern. One possibility is that learned information directly modifies or extends that in Conspec, while another is that they are totally dissociable. The second set of questions concerns the underlying neural structures, and the third concerns the relationship between species identification and learning the characteristics of individual members of a species. At this stage, we do not preclude the possibility that some species may possess more than one variety of Conlern mechanism. Let us first explore the characteristics of Conlern in the chick.

The Properties of Conlern in the Chick

How do the mechanisms and representations underlying Conlern relate to those involved in other kinds of learning?

Earlier, we reviewed evidence that the forebrain structure IMHV was crucial for the storage of information about an object following imprinting. Damage to IMHV resulted in impairments in acquiring information about both artificial and hen-like objects. The question remains, however, whether the integrity of the region is crucial in other learning situations. This question was initially investigated in a study in which chicks with their IMHV damaged were shown to be able to do a pattern discrimination task.[17] The task involved chicks being allowed to choose which of two alley-ways to run down. At the end of each alley-way there was a bright pattern. Approaching one of the patterns resulted in the chicks being rewarded by a puff of warm air. Most chicks quickly learn to approach the particular one of the two patterns associated with the reward. It turns out that chicks without an IMHV learn the task just as quickly as do intact birds. IMHV, then, while being vital for the learning taking place during imprinting, is not the only site for visual learning in the chick.

Johnson and Horn[18] addressed the same question in a different way in a study in which both imprinting and associative learning were combined within the same task. Day-old, visually naïve chicks will quickly learn to press one of two pedals in order to be presented with an attractive stimulus.[19] As a chick learns to associate pressing the particular pedal with the presentation of an attractive object, it also learns about the visual characteristics of the object. This is shown in a subsequent choice test when the chick is given a choice between the reinforcing object and a novel object, and prefers the former. Since the two processes of recognition and association develop concurrently, this training procedure appeared to be an appropriate one to enquire whether or not the two processes could be dissociated by experimentally induced localized damage to IMHV.[20]

The operant training apparatus had two conspicuous checked-pattern pedals set into the floor (see figure 4.2). Three of the walls were

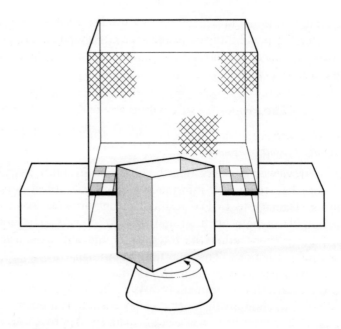

Figure 4.2   *Diagram of the operant training apparatus with one of the reinforcing stimuli in front of the open mesh side. The chick could depress the checked pedals by standing on them. Depressing one of the pedals resulted in the illumination and rotation of the stimulus. Depressing the other pedal had no effect. After Bateson and Reese (1969).*

painted black. The fourth was made of wire mesh so that the chick could see the reinforcing object when it was illuminated and rotating. This object, either the red box or the stuffed hen, would be illuminated and would start to rotate when a particular one of the two pedals was pressed. The chick could press a pedal merely by stepping on it. Often when a chick pressed a pedal and the stimulus appeared, the chick moved off the pedal in an attempt to approach the object. As a result the object ceased to be illuminated and stopped rotating. Pressing the other pedal had no effect. The chick, then, had to learn to step on the one pedal and not the other.

Chicks with damage to IMHV did not differ significantly from normal chicks in various measures of performance in the operant task: (1) in the mean latency to first pedal press, (2) in the percentage of birds in each group that reached the criterion of 9 out of 10 correct presses, (3) in the time taken to reach criterion, (4) in the time spent on the active pedal. Both groups of chicks reached criterion significantly more quickly in the second of the two training sessions than in the first. Two hours after the second training session in the operant training apparatus the chicks were given a choice test. In this test the chicks were able to approach either the object with which they had been rewarded during the operant task or a novel object. The normal control chicks preferred the object which had been used as the reinforcer. In situations like this it is well established that chicks will approach the more familiar of the two objects. In the course of learning the association, then, the normal chicks had also learned the characteristics of the reinforcing object. In contrast, the chicks with damage to IMHV showed no preference. This latter group of chicks were no less active during training or testing but, unlike the normal group, they did not direct their movements selectively toward the object seen previously. Thus, while being able to acquire the association between the pedal press and exposure to the object, they were subsequently unable to recognize the object.

It seems reasonable to assume that if imprinting and associative learning are subserved by the same mechanisms, then acquiring information about an object via one type of learning should reduce the amount of time taken to learn about the same object via the other. In other words, the characteristics of an object learned about in one situation do not have to be re-acquired in the other. However, if imprinting and associative learning are independent mechanisms, then there may be no transfer of information between the two. The available evidence supports this latter view. For example, Bateson and Reese[21] carried out an operant training task using the apparatus described earlier (shown in figure 4.2). They used two groups of birds which differed only in that one group had previously been exposed to the rewarding object (a rotating illuminated box) while the other group had not. The amount of exposure would have been sufficient to ensure that the birds were imprinted on to this object and would show a strong preference for it in a preference test. When they began the operant training task therefore, these birds must have already had a representation of the reinforcing object. If the same mechanisms underlie both imprinting and operant learning, then, this group of birds should have reached criterion faster than a group of birds not previously imprinted on the object. Bateson and Reese found that there were no differences between the groups in the speed of acquisition of the operant learning task. In this situation, knowledge about the characteristics of the reinforcing object does not help in the learning of an association involving it.

What about the converse situation? Namely, does the prior formation of associations involving an object facilitate the subsequent recognition of that object? This question was investigated by Bolhuis and Johnson[22] who studied two groups of chicks. One group, the 'response-contingent' group were trained to press a pedal in order to be exposed to an object. The second group of chicks did not have control over the presentation of the object, but were merely shown it whenever a partner 'response-contingent' bird pressed the pedal. Thus, although both groups were exposed to the stimulus object in an identical manner, in one group only was the object involved in the formation of an association. If associations involving an object facilitate its subsequent recognition then the 'response-contingent' group should have a higher preference for the rewarding object after operant training. This was not the case. Taken together, these neural and behavioural dissociations provide strong evidence that exposure learning can be dissociated from the formation of associations between representations.

Thus far, we have discussed the evidence for dissociations between the exposure learning subserved by IMHV and the neural systems underlying Conspec on the one hand, and associative learning on the other. However, it would be premature to conclude from this evidence that the learning system involved in imprinting is unique. A variety of possibilities remain regarding the range of other tasks in which the system might be involved. For example, we discussed in chapter three how the integrity of IMHV is essential for the recognition of the individual adult hen.[23] Is the region also involved in other tasks which require the recognition of individual conspecifics? This question has recently been investigated.

Animals of several species, when choosing a mate, prefer individuals which are slightly different, but not very different, from those with which they were reared, a phenomenon known as *optimal outbreeding*. This behaviour ensures that the animals' genes are combined with others that contain the same general adaptations, yet that are different enough to provide some variation.[24] In a recent experiment carried out at Cambridge University, normal female chickens were raised in small social groups with one male until they were three months old. When tested at this age the females preferred to approach and stand next to a novel male of the same strain rather than either the male with whom they had been reared, or a novel male of a novel strain. This selective approach behaviour is in accordance with optimal outbreeding. A second group of female chickens had their IMHV removed on their first day of life, and were subsequently reared in an identical manner to the normal chickens. Although the experimental birds appeared normal in most respects, they did not have a selective preference for any of the test males when they were tested at three months of age: one might conclude that they appeared to be incapable of discriminating between them[25] (see figure 4.3). The previous work had established that IMHV was the location where information was stored concerning the hen on which a chick had been imprinted. This would normally

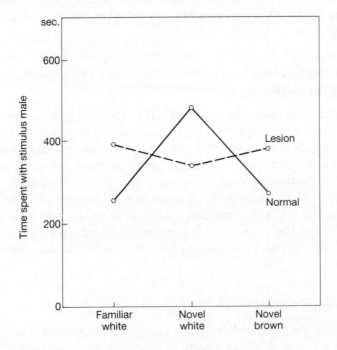

Figure 4.3 *Mean time spent by adult hens with lesions to IMHV and normal adult hens near particular male cocks. Each female was tested with a white male with which it had been reared, a novel white male and a novel brown male (different strain). Normal females spent significantly more time with the novel male of the same strain (optimal outbreeding). The birds with IMHV lesions showed no preference, suggesting that they were unable to recognize the characteristics of a particular individual of their own strain. From Bolhuis et al. (1989).*

have been the chick's own mother. The experiment just described demonstrates that IMHV is also involved in storing information concerning other individual conspecifics as well.

In this section we have described the particular properties of Conlern in the chick. The picture that one comes away with is that of a mechanism that functions independently of any other in the chick's brain. It is involved in the storage not only of descriptions of mother and other conspecifics, but also of other objects that the chick might be presented with in the first few days of life which have the movement normally characteristic of mother. This learning is purely passive and is engaged simply by exposure to the object. It is a specialized device and the information it possesses does not appear to be accessible by other systems.

Are the neural structures and pathways supporting Conlern the same as those supporting Conspec?

We have seen that the region IMHV in the chick forebrain is implicated in the acquisition and retention of information following imprinting. While damage to this area impairs both the acquisition and retention of preferences resulting from exposure to an object, a Conlern function, it does not impair the specific predisposition to approach objects resembling an adult hen, a property of Conspec.[26] That is, the effect of damaging IMHV is to *impair only the acquired component of filial preferences*. It may be concluded, then, that at least one of the neural structures critical for Conlern is not crucial for Conspec.

The recognition of species and individual members of a species

Originally, for Konrad Lorenz the function of imprinting was '. . . to establish a sort of consciousness of species in the young birds'. (see chapter three, box 3.1). The evidence we have presented in chapter three, however, supports the contention that the primary function of imprinting is to establish preferences for individual adult birds. Paradoxically, then, individual recognition may preceed species recognition rather than the other way round.

Conlern in the Human Infant

How do the mechanisms and representations underlying Conlern relate to those involved in other kinds of learning?

To our knowledge, there is no evidence from the human infant directly relevant to this issue. The evidence from adults, however, is broadly consistent with the notion that face processing does not depend upon unique neural or cognitive mechanisms. For example, the evidence on the 'inversion effect' mentioned in chapter two, leads one to the conclusion that other classes of stimuli in which subjects are as experienced are processed by similar types of mechanisms as are faces. Similarly, data from adult neuropsychology indicates that patients suffering from prosopagnosia, the inability to recognize faces, also have problems in identifying individual animals or objects (such as cars or handbags), though the precise nature of the problem may differ from individual to individual.[27] In the next chapter we enquire further into the nature of human Conlern.

Neuroanatomical pathways of Conspec and Conlern in the infant

Why is it that the tracking task discussed in chapter two is so effective in eliciting a discriminatory response to faces in new-borns? As we suggested earlier, saccadic pursuit tracking may be mediated largely by the subcortical visual pathway in the new-born. Thus, it appears plausible to propose that Conspec may be accessed primarily via the subcortical visual pathway. We reiterate at this point that we use the phrase the 'subcortical visual pathway' for ease of exposition, and that we are well aware that a simple dissociation between cortical and subcortical circuits is insufficient. That is, our statement that new-born tracking behaviour is primarily mediated by subcortical structures such as the superior colliculus does not mean that we wish to exclude some partial involvement of the deeper cortical layers. We expand upon this point in chapter six. Our claim is merely that new-born behaviour such as tracking is not controlled by the same full cortical mechanisms as it is in the adult. This conclusion is supported by the developmental time course of preferential tracking (see chapter five). Having said this, however, we see no reason to believe a priori that subcortical structures such as the superior colliculus are incapable of the level of complexity of information processing required to support a Conspec device.

Over the first month or so of life, the infant spends a lot of time looking at faces due, we argue, to Conspec. It is possible that the cortical circuits which support Conlern configure themselves appropriately for processing information about the detailed characteristics of the human face in response to this exposure. As we discussed in the previous chapter, around the second or third month of life cortical circuits begin to gain increasing control over the infant's visuospatial responses. As the circuits underlying Conlern mature, the infant begins to attend longer to faces than to other stimuli in the infant-control testing procedure. The infant-control procedure is sensitive to this mechanism since it involves static presentations within the central visual field and, as we mentioned earlier, foveal retinal cells feed mainly into the cortical visual pathway. Thus, we may suppose that Conspec and Conlern in the human infant may have dissociable neural substrates.

What does Conlern learn about?

It is clear that infants learn something about the properties of faces over the first two months of life. This was demonstrated clearly in a study by Kleiner and Banks,[28] who tested eight week-old infants with the stimuli shown in figure 4.1. There were three differences between the results for these infants and those reported by Kleiner for new-borns.[29] As discussed earlier, the newborns preferred the crossed stimulus with the amplitude spectrum of the face (Af/Pl) to the one with the phase spectrum of the face (Al/Pf). By two months of age, however, this preference had reversed. In addition, there was no preference between the crossed stimulus with the amplitude of the face (Af/Pl) and the lattice (Al/Pl), whereas the former was preferred by new-borns. Finally, while the new-borns had treated the lattice (Al/Pl) and the crossed stimulus with the amplitude of the lattice (Al/Pf) as equivalent, the two-months-olds preferred the latter.

Kleiner and Banks[30] summarize the differences between new-borns and two-month-olds in the following way:

> Neonates' preferences appear to be based on stimulus energy, as indexed by the amplitude spectrum, whereas some two-month-olds' preferences seem to be based on stimulus structure as indexed by the phase spectrum.

We discussed the interpretation of the neonate data in an earlier section of this chapter, concluding that while stimulus energy, as indexed by the amplitude spectrum, might be the correct account of neonate preferences for stimuli other than faces, Kleiner's own data suggest most strongly that the neonate possesses structural information about faces. In the above quotation, Kleiner and Banks are attempting to maintain a form of the sensory hypothesis with the two-month-olds. Rather than the crucial variable being the amplitude spectrum of the stimulus, however, it is the *phase spectrum*.

This phase spectrum theory would predict that there would be no preference expressed at two months of age between the face (Af/Pf) and the crossed stimulus with the phase of the face (Al/Pf), since they share the phase spectrum of the face. In fact, the infants still overwhelmingly preferred the face stimulus (Af/Pf). It cannot be argued that such a preference is the consequence of the summing of preferences driven by phase and by amplitude spectra, since amplitude spectra seem to be playing no role at all in the preferences of the two-month-old infants in this experiment. This follows from the fact that at two months of age the infants have no preference between the two stimuli with the phase of the lattice (Af/Pl and Al/Pl). The only option for a sensory hypothesis, then, would be to say that the amplitude spectrum influenced preferences only if the stimulus had the phase spectrum of a face. Since the phase spectrum of the face is, arguably, more complex computationally than the face itself, it seems much more parsimonious to propose that, by two months, Conlern has learned something about the structure of the face which is not meaningfully decomposable into phase or amplitude spectra. We assume that what is learned has to do with the features of the face and their relationships.

Our characterization of what Conlern has learned by two months of age is of the same general form as our characterization of the contents of Conspec. However, there are differences between them. This is illustrated most clearly in these experiments in the difference in reaction by new-borns and two-month-olds to the crossed stimulus with the phase spectrum of the face (Al/Pf). Our adult perceptual processes can pick out a face from the stimulus, and the data obtained by Kleiner and Banks indicates that the two-month-old infant can do likewise. The data obtained with new-borns, however, indicates that the Conspec mechanism cannot detect any facedness in this crossed stimulus, since they showed no preference between it and the lattice

(Al/Pl). The new-borns, then, responded to these two stimuli solely on the basis of their amplitude spectra: Conspec was not engaged by either of them.

The Interaction between Conlern and Conspec

There are a number of options for the interaction between Conlern and Conspec. We will confine ourselves to discussing three possibilities, which are also illustrated in figure 4.4:

1 There is no direct internal interaction between Conlern and Conspec. While both systems influence the overall behaviour of the animal, they do so quite independently. If this were the case then the only interaction between the two systems occurs *via the external environment*. This would be the case if the only function of Conspec is to orient the animal toward any face-like stimuli in the external environment. Conlern, then, can be allowed to acquire information about the characteristics of any object to which it is exposed. Conlern will learn about faces by virtue of the animal being oriented toward them very frequently.
2 Conspec acts as a sensory filter which selects the information allowed to pass through to Conlern. Conlern acquires information about faces because that is the only class of stimulus allowed to pass through Conspec. Note that this form of interaction is related to the notion of a 'template' introduced by Peter Marler and others.[31]
3 Conspec has a regulatory function over Conlern. In this type of interaction Conspec neither controls attention nor does it filter the input to Conlern, but it issues a functional <learn how> signal to Conlern whenever a stimulus which matches Conspec is present.

The Locus of the Interaction Between Conspec and Conlern in the Chick

In recent years, one of the areas of focus of the Cambridge laboratory has been to unravel the nature of the interaction between the specific predisposition (Conspec) and imprinting (Conlern). Let us first examine interaction type (2) where Conspec acts as a sensory filter. If this were the correct view of the role of Conspec then we should expect to find sharp restrictions on what a chick could learn as a function of the

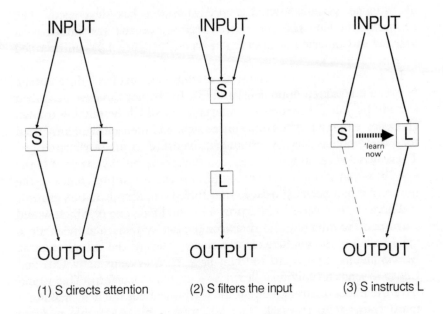

Figure 4.4   *A schematic illustration of three ways that Conspec and Conlern could interact (see text for further details). S = Conspec and L = Conlern.*

emergence of the Conspec predisposition. Prior to the emergence of the predisposition, all suitable stimuli (i.e. of the appropriate size and with appropriate movement) would pass through to Conlern, and so a red box would be as easy to learn about as a hen. Thus far the theory corresponds to the available data. However, once the predisposition has matured in Conspec, only stimuli with correct head and neck would be allowed through to Conlern. At this stage, then, the chick would not be able to imprint onto the red box.

In a recent series of experiments, Bolhuis, Johnson and Horn[32] tested this prediction by allowing Conspec to develop in dark-reared chicks using the procedures described in chapter three. In one of these experiments a group of chicks with Conspec activated were trained by exposure to either the red box or the blue box, after which their preferences were measured in a choice test. Preference tests revealed a significant preference for the training object in both groups of chicks. This result, and those of three other similar experiments, clearly indicated that chicks are capable of learning about the characteristics of artificial stimuli after the predisposition has developed. The properties of Conspec, do not, therefore, restrict the information arriving at Conlern and interaction type (2) (figure 4.4) can be ruled out for the chick.

In a very recent experiment an attempt was made to differentiate between interaction options (1) and (3). In chapter three we described a study by Johan Bolhuis and colleagues in which he initially trained chicks on either a red box or a stuffed hen, and then subsequently tried to reverse preferences by prolonged exposure to the other stimulus. There was a reversal of preference in the group initially exposed to the box (box–hen group), but not significant change in preference in the group that had been exposed to the stuffed hen first (hen–box group).

There are two ways to interpret these findings, one of which would correspond to interaction (1) between the two systems, and the other to (3). Account (3) would run as follows. During the initial training period chicks exposed to the hen have both systems activated, and Conspec sends a functional 'learn how' signal to Conlern. This would have the effect of strengthening the learning about the hen, making it more resistant to reversal. The box-trained birds are able to learn about the box. However, without the addition of a signal from Conspec, the learning is fragile and easily reversed. This is an additional assumption required for this account to work. The alternative, type (1) account, is that during training on day one Conspec is not yet active (this is what we might expect from the studies reported in chapter three). Thus, in both groups of birds, only Conlern is active at this stage. By day two, Conspec has developed (again corresponding to our expectations from the studies described earlier) and exerts an influence on preference behaviour in the test by shifting all preferences toward the hen.

A recent experiment suggests that the latter account (corresponding to a type (1) interaction between Conspec and Conlern) is more plausible.[33] In this experiment advantage was taken of the fact that dark-reared chicks require some motor activity within 12 to 36 hours after hatching in order for Conspec to develop (see chapter three). If option (3) is correct, then the differential reversibility will be observed even when the whole experiment is conducted after the emergence of Conspec. If option (1) is correct then differential reversibility should be observed only when training and testing times are such that Conspec is emerging between the first and second preference tests. The evidence available so far is consistent with the predictions of interaction type (1): that there is no internal interaction between Conspec and Conlern in the chick.

The Locus of the Interaction Between Conspec and Conlern in the Human Infant

We have argued for a separate neural substrate for the two systems in the human, and further evidence for this will be presented in the next chapter. To our knowledge, however, there is no evidence available at present that would allow us to discriminate among the three options for interaction among them in the human infant. This remains a challenge for future research.

At the beginning of this chapter we presented three conclusions from our earlier discussion. Based on the conclusions from the biological evidence reviewed in chapter three, we have argued in this chapter for a two-process theory of the development of face recognition. In brief, we have demonstrated that infants are born with some knowledge concerning the visual structure of the human face. This is the Conspec mechanism. The effect of Conspec is to cause the infant to orient towards any stimuli fitting its specification. Dissociable from Conspec is Conlern. In the absence of evidence to the contrary we postulate that for the human infant Conlern learns about faces effectively merely because the infant pays a lot of attention to them (type (1) interaction).

So far we have only discussed human Conspec and Conlern in the broadest of terms. In the next chapter we investigate the nature of these structures in the human in more detail.

5

Conspec and Conlern in the Human Infant

Further Studies on Human Conspec

We extended our investigations into the nature of 'Conspec' in the human infant by conducting experiments on three issues:

1 Which characteristics of the schematic face engage Conspec?
2 What is the developmental time course of Conspec?
3 Given that Conspec cannot be accounted for in terms of the linear systems model (LSM), how do these two mechanisms interact to influence the new-born's behaviour?

The Contents of Conspec

We argued in the previous chapter that the human infant seems to possess a Conspec: that is, a *primal* specification of some structural characteristics of the human face. We wished to explore further the properties of human Conspec, and Suzanne Dziurawiec, who ran the Aberdeen new-born study discussed in chapter two, joined us in London to help us do so. We knew that Conspec provides sufficient information to allow an infant to prefer a normal over a scrambled schematic face. However, there is a good deal of leeway in the specification which would allow this discrimination. For example, the infants could have been simply responding to the three high-contrast areas, 'blobs', that constitute the configuration or arrangement of features which comprise a face. Assuming lighting from above, a real human face may be identified by the area of shadow around the eyes and mouth. In the next experiment we wanted to investigate which aspects of the face stimulus used in the earlier study were responsible

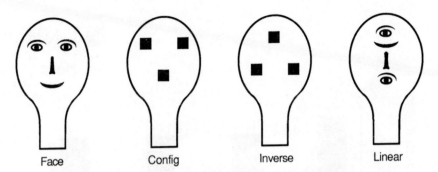

Face   Config   Inverse   Linear

Figure 5.1   *The four stimuli used in the new-born study.*

for attracting the new-borns' attention.[1] Accordingly, we included a stimulus that we considered to be the minimum structural specification for Conspec: three dark squares in the appropriate locations for the eyes and mouth regions. If the new-borns are using the configuration of high-contrast elements to track faces then the realistic face should not be preferred over this stimulus. As a control stimulus we used a similar but inverted pattern. Note that any stimulus has the same amplitude spectrum (see chapter 4, box 4.1) irrespective of its orientation. The stimuli we used are shown in figure 5.1.

The sample consisted of 43 new-borns from the delivery ward of the Obstetrics Department of University College Hospital, London. They were tested at between 15 and 69 minutes after birth. The tracking procedure employed was identical to that described in chapter two, except that four rather than three stimuli were used. In addition, the infant lay in a purpose-designed holder with a head rest that fitted on the experimenter's lap. The mean head and eye turning as the infants attempted to track the four stimuli are shown in figure 5.2. For eye turning, the tracking of the schematic *face* was significantly greater than the response to *linear* or to *inverse*. The infant responses to *config* were anomalous. Some infants followed it as much as they did *face*; some treated it like a non-face. In consequence we could not find a reliable difference between *config* and *face*. Head turning did not discriminate the stimuli. Although the eye movement data has now been replicated in three different infant populations, whether new-borns will reliably turn their heads further to follow a moving face is still an open question.

As the eye movement data reported in the Goren study has now been replicated three times, we feel confident in concluding that infants in

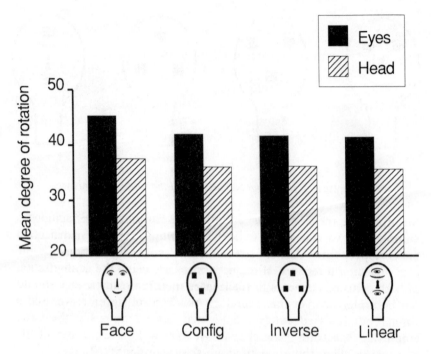

Figure 5.2   *The mean head and eye tracking of the four stimuli.*

the first hour of life are sensitive to the structure of the human face to some degree of detail. The lack of significant difference between *face* and *config* prevents us from concluding that Conspec is specified in more detail than three high-contrast blobs. The data obtained from this and the earlier experiments support the result of Goren and her colleagues, and strengthen the argument for a fairly complex perceptual organization being present at birth. Moreover, the argument that faces are special objects in the newborn's visual world gets further qualified support. It can now be accepted with some degree of confidence that neonates do find slowly moving faces with high contrast definition particularly attractive stimuli. That is not to say, however, that neonates have any conception of the meaning of a face. All that can be said is that they prefer to track a pattern that has face-like properties. In other words, performance need not be 'cognitive' in basis but could merely be like a sensory motor reflex.

The Time Course of Conspec

We have suggested that Conspec may be primarily mediated by subcortical structures and is independent of the mechanisms underlying Conlern. It has been postulated that, following maturation of various cortical pathways at around two months old, the control of visual attention passes to mechanisms accessed via the retinocortical pathway.[2] Two things follow from this. The first is that the preferential tracking of faces should decline at around this age. Prior to two months, Conspec should still be capable of controlling behaviour. As we have already noted, many authors have failed to find a face preference at one month. However they all used types of preference test that we argue are mediated by Conlern, a cortical mechanism. In order to engage Conspec we would need to use a task which can be mediated by subcortical circuits. Using such a task, we would expect to be able to find differential responding to faces at an age where everyone else has failed – at around one month. In order to investigate these issues we decided to study the tracking of face-like stimuli over the first five months of life.

In pilot studies we discovered that it was impossible to use the new-born tracking technique with infants of one month or older. They either attempted to reach for the stimulus, or got fussy because they preferred to be upright, or tracked all stimuli to the maximum extent. We therefore had to devise a version of the new-born tracking task for the older infants. After some time, we hit on the idea of rotating the infant in relation to the stimulus rather than moving the stimulus in relation to the infant, as in the new-borns. A special rotating chair apparatus was built for the purpose. The stimulus was in a fixed location so that when the chair turned the babies had to turn their head and eyes in order to keep the stimulus in view. Thus the technique is a tracking task which is equivalent to that used successfully with new-borns. The babies sat on the lap of a trained holder about 90 cm. from a rear projection screen. The holder sat on a specially designed chair that rotated away from the screen (see figure 5.3). We used the same four stimuli that had been used in an earlier experiment (see figure 2.6): a schematic face (*face*), *config*, the stimulus with rearranged features (*linear*), and a stimulus composed of the elements of facial features scattered around symmetrically (*scrambled*). These stimuli were presented twice, initially in random order and then in reverse order. The procedure which followed was similar in some respects to that described above. Briefly, this involved showing one of the four stimuli on the projection screen. After five seconds a motor that rotated the chair was switched on and the chair began to rotate such that the infant was slowly moved away from the stimulus (see figure 5.3). The infants turned their heads to keep the stimulus in view. We presume that the more interesting the stimulus was, the more an infant would turn its head. Eventually all the infants stopped looking at the stimulus and returned their heads to a forward gaze. After the chair had rotated through 90 degrees, it returned to the starting position ready for the next trial. When the four stimuli had been tested in this way, the process was repeated with the chair rotating in the opposite direction. For the entire experiment the infant's face and the timer were recorded on videotape. Further, the length of time that the infant had looked at each slide was later assessed by a judge who did not know which stimuli were being shown.

We used three groups of subjects: 38 infants aged approximately one month old, 16 three-month-olds and 16 five-month-olds. The mean angle of the chair at which infants stopped looking at the slides for the

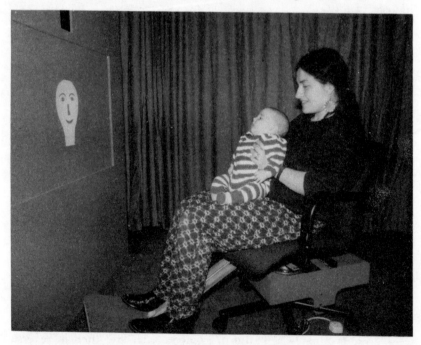

Figure 5.3   *The moving chair apparatus used in the infant study.*

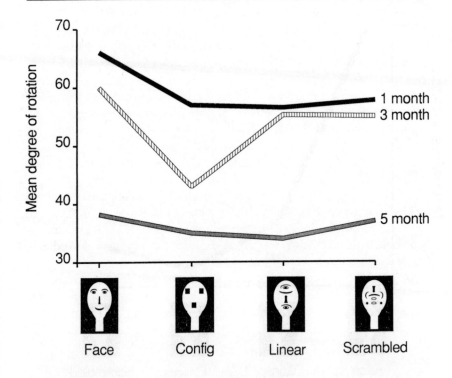

Figure 5.4 *Mean chair angle at disengagement from each of the four stimuli for the three age groups.*

three age groups is shown in figure 5.4. For the three- and five-month-old groups of infants there was no effect of stimulus on chair angle when the infant looked away.[3] *Config* was followed less than the other stimuli, but the difference was not significant. With the infants around one month old there was a statistically significant effect of stimulus on the amount of tracking. Furthermore, individual statistical comparisons revealed that the face was tracked significantly further than all of the other stimuli.

The results were consistent with the existence of a decline in the preferential tracking of faces between one and three months of age. In an attempt to pin down further the age when the influence of Conspec declines, we took advantage of our fairly wide age range in the group of infants around one month and further sub-divided the group into an 'older' and 'younger' sub-group. When we analysed the results from these two groups separately, only in the 'younger' group was the face

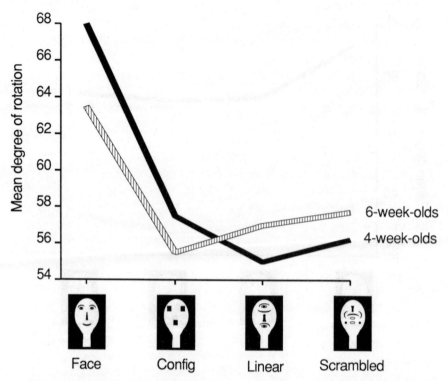

Figure 5.5 *Mean chair angle at disengagement from each of the four stimuli for the four- and six-week-old groups.*

significantly preferred over the other stimuli (see figure 5.5). This *post hoc* finding strongly implies that the preferential tracking of face declines between four and six weeks after birth. This decline is a little earlier than the decline of some other subcortically controlled behaviours,[4] but is well within the required period.

In the Goren study, and in our replication reported in chapter two, it has been established that, using a tracking task, new-borns turn further to look at normally configured faces than at scrambled faces. Earlier, we also described how the results of several other studies had indicated that faces are not preferentially attended to until the infants are about two months old. The present experiment establishes that the apparent discrepancy in the data relates to the testing method used. Although one-month-old infants show no preference for faces in the infant control procedure (argued to be primarily cortically mediated), they do show a face preference in a tracking task (argued to be primarily subcortically mediated). We have, therefore, been able to confirm one prediction of the two-process theory put forward in the last chapter. The data thus far are consistent with the theory that Conspec is primarily subcortically mediated while Conlern is primarily cortically mediated and that the switch from subcortical to cortical control takes place at some time during the second month of life.

The possibility remains that Conspec could still be active, and thus preferential orienting to faces could still be found in infants of three months of age and older if an even more sensitive testing technique could be found. The problem with the moving chair design is that as the infants get older they start to track the stimuli smoothly. The experiment then becomes a test of the foveal-cortical system with a moving stimulus. With this in mind, we designed a variant of the moving chair apparatus in which the infant was required to orient toward a stimulus appearing in the peripheral visual field. Within the theory we have proposed, Conspec should be most effective when the stimuli are presented in the peripheral visual field (see p. 137). The modified orienting technique makes this possible.

The procedure for this experiment was similar to that for the previous one except that the chair began its rotation at 90 degrees to the screen where the stimulus was presented. The chair was then rotated such that this angle was slowly reduced. When the infant was attending to an attractor stimulus directly in front of it (and attached to the end of the chair), the test stimulus was presented on the screen (at 90 degrees to the infant's central line of vision) and the chair started to rotate the infant toward the screen. At a certain point, usually between 30 to 50 degrees from the starting point, the infant would disengage its attention from the attractor stimuli and orient toward the test stimulus in its peripheral visual field. As soon as the infant disengaged from the central stimulus to attend toward the peripheral one, the chair stopped rotating and returned to its starting location. Half of the trials began at 90 degrees to the right and half at 90 degrees to the left.

We tested 25 infants of three months of age and 25 infants of five months of age. The results are shown in figure 5.6. In neither of these age groups did the infants orient significantly sooner toward the face than toward the other stimuli. This result then, although suffering the weakness of all negative results, is consistent with the conclusion that the preferential orienting toward face stimuli in the peripheral visual field has disappeared by three months of age and that, accordingly,

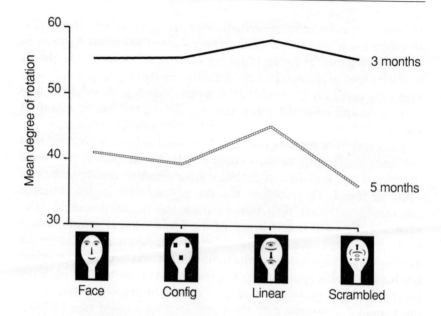

Figure 5.6 *Mean chair angle at orienting toward the four test stimuli for three- and five-month-olds.*

Conspec no longer exerts an influence on behaviour, even under optimal conditions.[5]

Conspec and the Linear Systems Model

As mentioned earlier, for the first few months of life, infants' preferences for a variety of patterns, including checks, bull's-eye targets and stripes, are well predicted by the linear systems model or LSM.[6] This model holds that new-borns' pattern preferences are influenced only by the amplitude spectrum (see chapter four, box 4.1 for more details).

In chapter four we discussed the study by Kathleen Kleiner[7] which was designed to test neonates' preferences among face-like and abstract patterns in the context of the linear systems model. One of the crucial comparisons in Kleiner's study was between a schematic face and a crossed stimulus made up from the amplitude spectrum of the face and the phase spectrum from another stimulus (see figure 4.1). In the condition using the two crucial stimuli, the new-borns overwhelmingly preferred the face. We argued that this finding indicates that there is no way in which new-borns' reactions to faces could be accounted for solely on the basis of the amplitude spectrum of the stimuli. Since the LSM operates only on the basis of amplitude spectrum, it cannot predict this result.

We are not challenging the validity of LSM with respect to stimuli other than faces. On the contrary, the LSM theory has proved most fruitful, unifying a range of data which had previously been explained only by a discordant set of *ad hoc* theories. Our claim is simply that faces are special for the new-born in the sense that the human infant also possesses a Conspec. How then might Conspec and LSM interact? In collaboration with Daphne Maurer[8] we have proposed that they could operate in parallel. The way this would work is as follows. Basically, the LSM claims that the early parts of the visual system act as a filter, restricting the energy which gets through to influence behaviour to that below a certain frequency cut-off point. In the LSM, all the energy getting through to the decision point is summed. This will take place separately for different parts of the visual field. At any instant, then, the infant's attention will be directed towards that part of the visual field containing most energy. At the same time, we believe, Conspec responds to those stimuli which impinge on the peripheral visual field and which possess certain characteristics. In fact, the function of Conspec is to direct the infant's attention to any faces in the vicinity. In a choice situation, the infant's behaviour would, therefore, be determined by some combination of the influence of the two mechanisms. If this is the case, then analysis of the filtered amplitude spectra of the stimuli used in the new-born studies we have described earlier should not conform strictly to predictions of the LSM. Specifically, the LSM should be able to predict the sequence of preferences for the non-face stimuli, but not the fact that the schematic face stimulus was most preferred. In order to test this, we analysed all the test stimuli used in the earlier new-born studies.[9] In figure 5.7 we show our analysis of the amplitude spectra of the stimuli used in Kleiner's study.

Our analysis of Kleiner's stimuli broadly confirmed that the LSM could predict the preference for the face over the lattice on the assumption that the upper cut-off for the LSM filter is less than 0.3 cycles/degree (to the left of 0.3 in figure 5.7). As mentioned earlier, however, LSM could not predict Kleiner's finding of a preference for the face over the crossed stimulus with the amplitude of the face and the phase of the lattice. Since these stimuli had the same amplitude

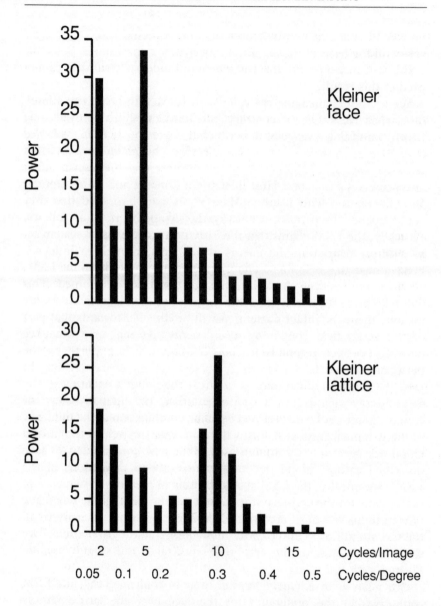

Figure 5.7   *Amplitude spectra for the stimuli used in the Kleiner (1987) study. 'Power' is given in arbitrary units. Values to the left correspond to large elements of the stimulus and values to the right correspond to small elements. The lattice has more small elements of a uniform size than does the face (see figure 4.1).*

spectrum, the LSM prediction is that they would be equally preferable.

In the next figure we illustrate the amplitude spectra for the stimuli used in the new-born tracking studies (see figure 5.8). These analyses provide further problems for the LSM. If the LSM were to account for the preference for *face* over *scrambled*, then it would have to exclude energy above 0.1 cycles/degree because of the energy peak in *scrambled* at that value. However, if the LSM filter were restricted to 0.05 to 0.1 cycles/degree we would have to predict that, in our second experiment, *config* and *inverse* would both be more attractive to new-borns than *face*. They are not, and, indeed, *inverse* is significantly less attractive. We conclude, then, once again, that LSM cannot account for the attractiveness of the face stimulus and that we need another mechanism to account for this.

As a result of the above analyses, it is apparent that the results obtained in the new-born tracking experiments cannot be ascribed to the frequency characteristics of the stimuli, and that the preference for the face is due to components of the stimulus not decomposable into amplitude spectra. In other words, this reanalysis of the test stimuli reinforces our conclusion from available data that Conspec is present in the human neonate.

So far we have looked only at experiments in which the face was the most preferred stimulus. If LSM operates in parallel with Conspec, however, it might be possible to design a stimulus optimal for the LSM which would elicit at least as much tracking as the face or even more. In the next experiment with new-born infants, we compared to the face and other stimuli a check pattern designed to have the optimal spatial frequency components for the new-born visual system.

For the new-born infant, the peak contrast sensitivity is between 0.1 and 0.2 cycles/degree.[10] Accordingly we chose to test infant tracking in response to a check pattern with an energy peak in this region. The stimuli employed were four head-shaped, head-sized, two-dimensional white forms about 17 x 19 cm. with black features. They were presented at approximately 18 to 25 cm. from the infant's face. The check stimulus was made up of 6 x 6 black and white squares of 2.25 cm. We also used the schematic *face* from earlier experiments and the *config* stimulus used in the previous experiments. In the previous experiment *config* was less attractive than *face* to new-borns. The final stimulus was a modification of *config* where the squares of the latter

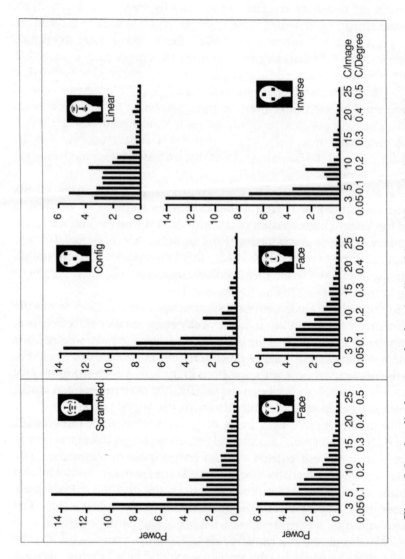

Figure 5.8 *Amplitude spectra for the stimuli used in tracking experiments with new-borns.*

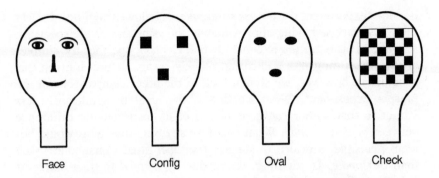

Figure 5.9   *The four stimuli used in the experiment of Morton, Bartrip and Johnson.*

were replaced by ovals. The four stimuli are shown in figure 5.9 and their amplitude spectra can be seen in figure 5.10.

Our sample consisted of 20 normal, healthy new-borns who were delivered at University College Hospital, London. The mean age at the start of testing was 21.5 hours (range 3–41 hours). As described previously, the experimenter shuffled the stimuli and presented them approximately 18 to 25 cm. from the infant's face. The extent to which the infant would track the four stimuli was assessed in exactly the same manner as before. The extent of following, measured in terms of degrees of arc, was determined by comparing the final nose position and eye orientation on each trial with the protractor demarcations. For each stimulus, the infant's score for both head and eye turning was the average of the largest turns the infant made to the two sides, with a theoretical maximum possible of 90 degrees for each stimulus.[11]

The data from this experiment are given in figure 5.11. Infants track the *check* stimulus significantly further than all the others as measured by eye or head movements. This is the result we anticipated on the basis of our expectation that the LSM mechanism could be more powerful than Conspec. Among the other stimuli, we see that *config* is more attractive than *face* in this experiment, though the difference between the two is not significant. This result, combined with the non-significant difference in the other direction in the previous experiment (see p. 106) leaves us unable to say a great deal about the specificity of Conspec. Let us assume that there is indeed no difference in the attractiveness of *face* and *config*. We now have reason to believe that the attractiveness of *config* is not due to LSM factors alone, since in the previous experiment the *inverse* stimulus was followed significantly less than *face* (*inverse* having approximately the same amplitude spectrum as *config*). It is tempting to conclude that Conspec specifies the simpler of the two stimuli *face* and *config*, namely *config*. Before drawing this conclusion, however, we should look at the other comparisons in the present experiment. What we find is that *oval* is significantly less attractive than either *config* or *face*. Let us focus on the difference between *oval* and *config*. What could we attribute this to? It would not seem plausible, a priori, to suggest that *oval* fitted Conspec less well than did *config*. If anything, we might expect *oval* to be a better fit (which is why we tried it in the first place). We have to conclude, then, that *config* is more attractive to the LSM mechanisms – that is it is more visible to the new-born infants than *oval*. Looking back at the amplitude spectra in figure 5.10 we can see that *config* does indeed have

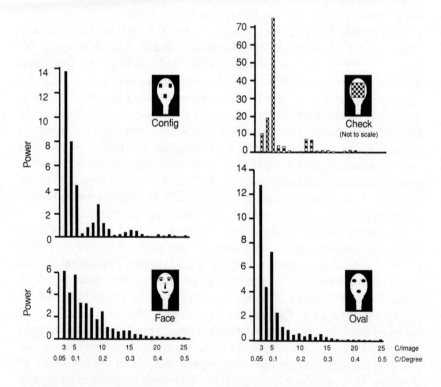

Figure 5.10   *The amplitude spectra of the four stimuli used in the experiment of Morton, Bartrip and Johnson.*

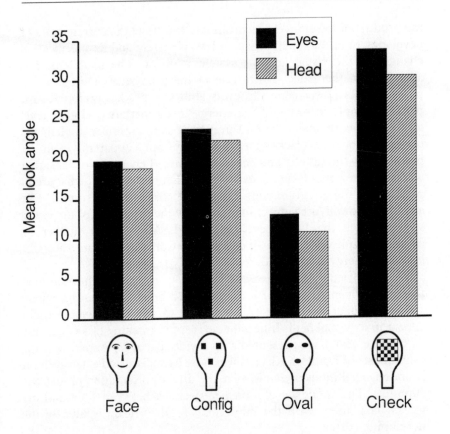

Figure 5.11 *The mean amount of tracking toward the four stimuli in the experiment of Morton, Bartrip and Johnson.*

more energy than *oval* in the region below 0.3 cycles/degree – the crucial region for the new-born infants. Overall, then, we take the results of this experiment as demonstrating that Conspec and LSM mechanisms are functioning in parallel. Both are necessary to describe the attractiveness of the stimuli we have used.

The reader may be tempted to enquire as to whether the LSM mechanism is thought to be cortical or subcortical. This would mistake its nature. As we understand Banks' conception, the LSM reflects the properties of the visual system, starting at the eye, proceeding through the retina and the early visual pathways to whatever mechanism or mechanisms currently controls attention for the infant. It is not itself a particular device with a particular evolutionary purpose but is rather the product of lower level specifications. It reflects the current state of development of the infant's visual nervous system and its specification changes as the visual nervous system matures. The model itself is actually a mathematical abstraction of the properties of these visual pathways. Its power comes from its ability to predict preference for patterns simply in terms of the energy in the patterns. Higher level terms such as symmetry or measures such as the number of elements or length of the black–white boundary can, apparently, all be predicted by the simpler and general measure of energy. Note also that when we claim that Conspec exists in parallel to the LSM, what are in parallel are the attention controlling mechanisms. Face stimuli, like any other stimuli, are subject to filtering by the properties of the visual system which the LSM describes. The LSM, however, makes its decision simply on the basis of energy, but Conspec takes into account how that energy is arranged.

We can briefly summarize our view of Conspec. We have argued that it is a primarily subcortically mediated *primal* mechanism which serves to direct the new-born's attention to any faces which might appear in its visual field. It becomes evident in tracking tasks or in any task where stimuli are presented with a wide spatial separation as in the experiments of Kathleen Kleiner, which we have discussed extensively. It is not engaged in tasks that involve the direct presentation of just one stimulus. The influence of Conspec declines between four and six weeks, coincident with the inhibition of subcortical circuits by the developing cortex.

Further Studies on Human Conlern

Moving Faces

In chapter two we referred to our findings in which five-month-old infants showed no preference for static schematic faces over scrambled faces, even in 'cortical' preference tests. A straightforward view of 'Conlern' might be that the more experience of faces the infant has, the more detailed will be its representation of what constitutes a face. Moreover, infants are interested in familiar stimuli and in novel stimuli. A static, simplified face-like stimulus would be neither familiar nor novel to a five-month-old. A familiar stimulus would be mother's face; a novel stimulus would be a scrambled face. If this line of reasoning is correct then we would expect that the simple monochromatic face stimuli used in the earlier studies may be insufficiently realistic to elicit preferential attention in older infants (five months). If this interpretation of the five-month-old result is correct, then restoring some of the characteristics of a real face to the simple schematic face should reinstate preferential attention toward the facial arrangement.

Among the most prominent characteristics of real faces is movement of the internal features. In a further experiment[12] we used the infant-control procedure to establish whether such movement would make a face-like configuration more attractive than the stimuli for the five-month-olds. We also tested groups of infants of one and three months of age.

The subjects were 25 one-month-olds, 22 three-month-olds and 18 five-month-olds, all normal, healthy, full-term births. The stimuli we used were all generated by a microcomputer and presented on a VDU. Three different configurations of facial features were used: *face*, *scrambled* and *linear* (see figure 5.12). For each of the three stimuli there were two conditions, *moving* and *static*. In the moving condition, the internal features of the face were made to move slightly by making transitions from one static presentation to another. The two frames alternated every second. The effect was one of animation of an otherwise constant stimulus. In the other, 'static' condition one of the two static frames for each configuration was presented. In total, therefore, each child was exposed to six stimuli, three static and three moving, presented in a random order.

The testing procedure was similar to that used in the 'infant-control' studies described in chapter two. The babies sat either on their parents lap or on the lap of a trained holder facing a VDU which was fitted behind a larger screen. The infants' eye movements were recorded by means of a video camera placed just below the VDU. The experimenter controlled the presentation of the stimuli by means of keys on a computer and began the session by presenting an attractor stimulus on the screen. Once the infant was attending to it, the experimenter pressed a key that caused the first test stimulus to appear. The test stimuli were presented in a random order determined by the computer. The experimenter watched a TV screen showing the infant's face and stopped the presentation of the first stimulus when the infant looked away from the screen for more than a second. The test stimulus was then replaced by an attractor pattern, and the next trial began in the same manner. Videotapes of the infants' eye

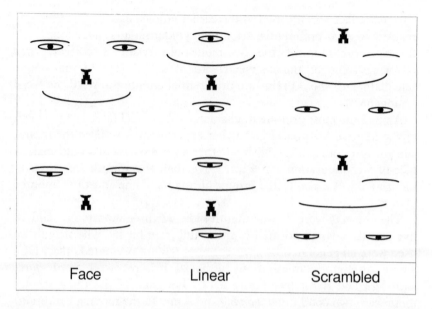

Figure 5.12 *The stimuli used in the 'moving faces' experiment. The effect of movement was achieved by making rapid transitions between the upper and lower frames.*

movements were subsequently coded by judges unaware of which stimuli were being presented.

Among one-month-olds, statistical analysis revealed no significant effect of stimulus on looking time. With the three-month-old group the face pattern was significantly preferred both in the static and in the moving conditions (figure 5.13). In figure 5.14 we show the mean values for the three configurations and two conditions for the group of five-month-olds. At this age there was no difference in the overall length of time the infants spent in looking at moving vs. static stimuli. For the static presentations there were no significant differences between the times spent looking at the three stimuli, whereas for the moving stimuli the face stimulus was significantly preferred over the other two.

The results obtained with the *static* patterns replicate those described in chapter two: while one- and five-month-olds show no significant preference for static *face* over the other static patterns, the three-month-olds did. This developmental pattern thus appears to be replicable across different stimulus presentation methods and viewing

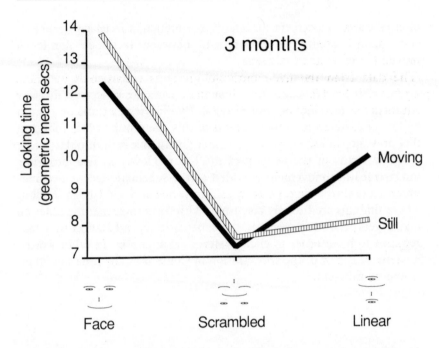

Figure 5.13   *The mean length of time spent looking at the stimuli when moving and when static for the three-month-old infants in the 'moving faces' experiment.*

distances and for white on black as well as black on white schematic faces. Even when the internal features are moving, one-month-olds show no evidence of a preference for a face-like arrangement of facial features. This result extends the claim made on the basis of earlier studies that, using preferential looking and habituation procedures, infants of around one month of age fail to show a preference for face-like arrangements. Only when the tracking technique is employed can a stimulus-initiated preference be demonstrated, as shown earlier in this chapter.

In the three-month-olds there was a significant effect of stimulus but no effect of movement and no interaction on an analysis of variance. Thus, while the configuration is important at this age, internal feature movement is not. While internal feature movement had no specific effects on the preferences of one- and three-month-olds, it did have a significant effect on the five-month-olds; the moving face pattern was significantly preferred over the two other moving stimuli. This finding is consistent with other recent reports indicating the importance of internal feature movement for infants' recognition of facial expressions,[13] and infants' ability to discriminate between facial or non-facial movement of abstract patterns.[14]

The data from the five-month-old group is consistent with the proposal that by this age static schematic faces are processed the way adults do: as face-like but not realistic. By this view, a static *face* could be less attractive than other stimuli to this age group, as we found in the previous infant-control experiment with five-month-olds (figure 5.6), by virtue of the novelty of the latter. However, if appropriate internal feature movement is added to the schematic face it becomes much more interesting, possibly as interesting as a real face in motion. These findings are broadly consistent with the notion that the older an infant gets, the more realistic the schematic representation of a face requires to be in order to elicit preferential attention. In other words, movement is part of the specification in Conlern by the time the infant is five-months-old.

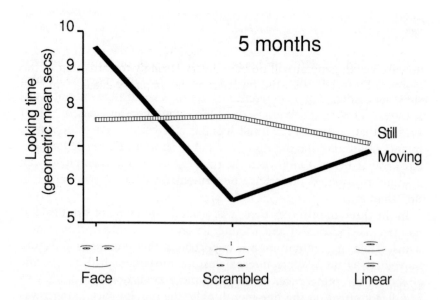

Figure 5.14 *The mean length of time spent looking at the stimuli when moving and when static for the five-month-old infants in the 'moving faces' experiment.*

Varieties of Conlern: Invariance Extraction and Individual Recognition

We have not yet addressed the question of what it is that the young of the species learns about faces. There are two different tasks which present themselves as possibilities. Let us talk about these in the context of the human infant. The first is to learn the characteristic of the human face in general. The advantage of this would be that the infant could distinguish any human, even a novel one, from any other being. The second is to learn the particular characteristics of father, mother or other primary caretaker, and to distinguish each of these from the others and any of them from any other humans. To a certain extent these two objectives are incompatible. In brief, a mechanism devoted to encoding the difference between humans and other beings has to discover what all human faces have in common. On the other hand, a device which is devoted to distinguishing between individuals has to be concerned with their dissimilarities rather than their similarities.

In practice, the distinction between these two kinds of mechanisms is not as simple as it first seems. We assume that the general *similarity* mechanism operates by averaging all the relevant stimuli it has encountered. If a new-born infant looks at mother's face two or three times more than at any other face, then its characterization of the human face in general will be biased very strongly towards that of the mother. Thus, although the function of the *similarity* mechanism may be to produce a representation of an average human face, if we attempted to test what the mechanism had encoded we would discover that it was largely based on the characteristics of the mother. We might, then, conclude that it was a mechanism of the second type, a *difference* mechanism, devoted to learning about individuals. If the primary function of the face-learning mechanism is to distinguish among individuals, the question arises of how to restrict what this mechanism learns about. Without such restrictions, it would also learn about any dogs, cats, horses or teddy bears that were in the environment. The restrictions would require to be implemented by a further mechanism whose function would be to let through only human faces. This latter mechanism would, thus, have to have a general specification of human faces to be able to do that job. That is, the 'filter' could be a mechanism of the 'similarity' detection kind.

This analysis assumes that the restrictions to Conlern are engineered by means of other visual cues. It would be possible for the device to respond to a non-visual cue, being guided by a principle such as 'only learn about things which talk'. There is, in addition, an empirical question as to whether young infants do indeed learn as much about dogs, cats and teddy bears as they do about the human beings in their environment. At present we do not know.

Let us now turn briefly to the equivalent evidence on Conlern in the chick. Note that it is possible for the first type of Conlern, the similarity detector, to retain information about specific individuals if its plasticity is terminated before it is exposed to more than one, or a few, faces. This is simply because the greater the number of individual faces such a system is exposed to, the more 'blurred' (incorporated into the average) the representation of any individual face will become. If there is no sensitive period for such a mechanism, then it will become a highly averaged 'template', and will eventually not be able to recognize individual faces, merely to discriminate human faces from other stimuli. Bearing this in mind, it seems reasonable to suppose that during imprinting a representation of an object is stored by the chick before the sensitive period 'self-terminates'. How, then, are we to account for all the evidence on the reversibility of imprinted preferences presented in chapter three? An experiment performed by Carel Ten Cate of Groningen University shed some light on this issue.[15]

Ten Cate studied sexual imprinting in two species of finch in order to make some inferences about the internal representation generated during this phase. Zebra finch males were sequentially imprinted to two different species of adult finch, the zebra finch and the Bengalese finch. When older these young males were given a preference test between the two species of finch and a third, hybrid of both species. If the young birds had separate representations of the two rearing species then they should have preferred these over the hybrid which they had never seen before. In contrast, if the young bird combined the representations from the two species then it might have been expected to prefer the hybrid over either of the rearing species. This, indeed, turned out to be the case. If the hybrid is preferred, it may be because the representations of the two species have been combined. While we acknowledge that there are difficulties in the interpretation of this experiment, it at least suggests that a 'similarity detector' may underlie imprinting. Thus, in the wild, the chick will be able to recognize its species by virtue of building up a representation of its mother. This does not mean that the representation is always linked to filial behaviour. Indeed, the representation will be used in other adult behaviour such as mate choice. Very few individuals other than mother may come to be recognized, and members of their own species outside that group would be treated as equivalent to members of other species.

In contrast to the chick, the human child comes to build up a vast library of familiar faces (up to several thousand according to some estimates). This obviously suggests that a Conlern mechanism is in operation which focuses on the differences between face exemplars rather than on their similarities. However, as argued earlier, such a mechanism may often require a *similarity* mechanism to provide a sensory template or filter. Without this tight constraint on input, a mechanism designed to focus on differences would absorb information about too wide a variety of inputs. Note that this is not a problem for the *similarity* Conlern since such a mechanism responds to the frequency of inputs: unlike the second type of mechanism it is not instance-based. That is, the first type of mechanism merely needs the majority of its inputs to be faces, or a particular face. The second type needs all its inputs to be within the class of faces. Given the computational need for one system to precede the other, is there any evidence for this developmental sequence in the human infant?

If a *similarity* Conlern existed then it would initially form a specification of the class 'face' on the basis of statistical regularities of the input. Which inputs it accepted would be guided initially by Conspec. There are two ways in which this could be done. First, it would be possible that only stimuli that satisfied Conspec would be accepted through to Conlern. Conspec would function as a 'print now' mechanism. An alternative would be a kind of boot-strap device. Under the influence of Conspec, the new-born infant pays far more attention to faces than to any other kind of stimulus. Conlern would initially learn about everything to which the infant paid attention. After a period of this (maybe only a few days) it could have built up enough information about the structure of the human face to serve as a filter itself. Since the mother's face is commonly the most frequently attended to, then we should expect such a system to be manifest as a preference for mother's face over other faces. That is, the mechanism would only have the capacity for storing an averaged representation – mainly mother plus some elements of father, siblings etc. This idea gives rise to the prediction that mother recognition should be possible in early infancy, but may subsequently show a decline as the mechanism becomes 'saturated'.[16] Father's face, although possibly preferred to other male faces, would not be preferred over a strange woman's face, since (usually) the face of the strange woman would share more characteristics in common with the mother.

Recognition of Mother

Ian Bushnell and colleagues[17] at the University of Glasgow have recently attempted to replicate, under more stringent conditions, a result originally reported by Tiffany Field[18] – that infants in the first few days of life will look at their mother more than a strange female face. Bushnell brought the mother, and another mother from the same hospital ward, into an experimental room. He located them such that their heads poked through a screen about 30 cms apart. The infant was then brought upright from a supine position and directed toward the screen with the two faces. The infant's looking was recorded until it had clocked up 20 seconds of looking toward one or both of the faces. The mother and the stranger then changed their locations and the procedure was repeated. The results indicated that a small, but significant, preference for looking toward the mother was present (about 60 per cent). This result seemed to us very surprising – as it has to most people working with infants. If it proved replicable then we would have to think very carefully about how such an ability fitted in to the systems we have postulated. We have, therefore, embarked on a replication and extension of Bushnell's data in collaboration with Scania de Schonen in Marseilles. Initial findings suggest that the Bushnell result is, indeed, replicable.

These results, then, would suggest that a *similarity* Conlern mechanism may be operating from early in the infant's life. We would, however, predict that this preference for mother should decline before the human Conlern proper, capable of distinguishing among individuals, begins to function around the second month of life. These experiments are in progress in London.

6
Biology, Cognition and Faces

In chapter one we discussed two general ways in which evidence from biology might inform our thinking about cognitive development. The first was to consider evidence from ethology. In subsequent chapters, adopting this approach caused us to consider the environment of the young infant, and to consider evidence from other species in some detail. The second way that we argued information from biology could influence thinking about cognitive development came from studying postnatal growth of the brain. Taking this type of evidence more seriously influenced both the types of cognitive mechanism that we proposed and our thinking about the transitions between these mechanisms during development. In this final chapter we return to some of the general issues explored in chapter one in the light of the specific theoretical account we have given about the development of face recognition. We began by considering the ethological influences on our thinking. This led us to specify in a single conceptual framework a number of levels of environmental influence together with their products. It is within this framework that the comparative studies are easiest to understand.

An Ethological Framework

In thinking about development we have found it useful to locate the various constructs in our theory in relation to what is sometimes called the nature–nurture divide. The term *innate* is often used in the classical nature–nurture debates to refer purely to the genetic endowment. However, following Oyama, we can find no use for terms that are so restricted, since it is clear that one cannot meaningfully separate out the influence of the genome from that of certain aspects of the environment. Neither can we consider the internal environment alone. Many aspects of neural development cannot be made sense of without specifying the external stimuli that are expected in the course of this development, for these external stimuli help to shape the final form of the neural structures. It is at this point that our distinction between the 'species-typical environment' (STE) and the 'individual-specific environment' (ISE) becomes vital. The species-typical environment includes those external stimuli that all young of the species would be expected to encounter. As an example, the development of Conspec only requires the chick to be allowed a period of time to run about. The form of Conspec and the nature of the experience have no specific relationship. In contrast to this, the chick acquires information about what its species looks like through specific experience or learning. Members of its species would also be part of the chick's species-typical environment, but there is clearly a difference of kind between such specific stimulation and the motor experience required for Conspec. Thus, it turns out to be necessary to make a further sub-division within the species-typical environment between non-specific and specific stimulation. Another example of non-specific stimulation is the finding by Gottlieb, discussed in chapter three, that mallard chicks need to hear contentment calls for their species auditory preference to mature. The contentment calls are (so far as we know) non-specific with respect to the adult calls the chicks come to discriminate between without experience.

This division between specific and non-specific aspects of the species-typical environment turns out to be essential in helping us to delineate types of process that result from development. In table 6.1 we have listed the levels of the environment that we have found it

Table 6.1   Levels of interaction between genes and the environment

Sources of influence	Terms	
Genome	genetic	
Internal environment	innate	
Species-typical environment; non-specific stimulation	primal	
Species-typical environment; specific stimulation	normal	'learning'
Individual-specific environment		'learning'

useful to distinguish among together with terms that we or others have used to describe elements at that level.

We have used the term 'primal' to contrast with 'innate' and with 'learned'. Structures or processes have been defined as *primal* if they arise from the interaction of the genome with the internal environment and with non-specific external environmental input. Thus we would characterize Conspec in the chick as being *primal*. In addition, the call preference that develops in the mallard chick would also count as *primal* since the stimulation required was unrelated to the structures whose maturation it triggered.

The next level of environmental interaction, which includes the whole of the species-typical environment is vitally important if one is to understand the nature of the species in question. One can think of the genome as a plan which can only be understood in the context of the 'normal' environment. But the normal environment for a particular species includes not only the internal environment together with non-specific species-typical external environmental input but the specific aspects of the species-typical environment as well. Some learning can be seen as essential if the young creature is to develop within what we might call the normal developmental system. It is interactions through to the species-typical environment which gives rise to a normal developmental path.

The terms in the table are more or less productive in their use. The 'primal environment' is an expression of everything up to and including the non-specific aspects of the species-typical environment. That is, everything that can contribute towards a *primal* structure or process. The 'normal environment' is the name used for all environmental influences up to and including the species-typical environment.

Throughout the book we have focused on how the infant learns to recognize its own species and its mother in particular. This end is accomplished in very many species. One could regard the need to ensure that the infant comes to recognize its own species, then, as a particular biological task. Our discussion has shown that this task could be accomplished either by the use of a specific *primal* structure or by a non-specific structure together with a particular, specific species-typical environment.[1]

Conspec, Conlern and the Species-Typical Environment

We have suggested that the cognitive systems Conspec and Conlern make up an integrated developmental system in interaction with the species-typical environment. Both for humans and for the chick we concluded that only Conspec contained *primal* information about faces. Of course we do not believe that such mechanisms are restricted to the human and to the domestic fowl. Rather, we imagine that the majority of mammalian and avian species need to learn to recognize their own species and individuals within their species. The label 'Conspec' might predispose one to think in terms of a specification of facial features sufficiently detailed to discriminate the species from any other. However, we have already observed that for the human infant and for the chick, Conspec is very schematic. It is only in combination with the STE that Conspec can do the job that its name invokes.[2] In general, we anticipate that the specificity or otherwise of Conspec in any particular species, and the details of its interaction with Conlern, will depend crucially on characteristics of the STE. To illustrate this we return to some of the examples mentioned in chapter three.

The cuckoo has a particularly odd STE since it is reared by a host species and brought up with host-species chicks. However, as with any other bird, it has to be able to recognize its own conspecifics for breeding. In other species, approaches to prospective mates may be informed by Conlern. This, however, would not be adaptive within the cuckoo's STE since the cuckoo has no opportunity of learning about its own species until it leaves the nest. Because of its STE, then, the cuckoo may well have a visual Conspec,[3] which is very detailed and furthermore is not activated until after it leaves the nest. Conlern may have some role, however, since cuckoos often specialize in parasitizing the host species by which they were raised.[4]

Another example of the need to consider the relationship between the STE and the role of Conspec comes from contrasting two species of monkey. In chapter three we discussed how Japanese macaques are raised in troupes that intermingle with other monkey species. In contrast, rhesus macaques are raised in groups isolated from other species. Thus, the STE of the young monkeys differs in a significant way. The rhesus infants can learn about the characteristics of its own species by experience since it will rarely be exposed to any others which are closely related. The Japanese macaque, on the other hand, has to be able to discriminate its own species from the others with which it is reared. It is likely that information about the facial characteristics of its own species would be specified in Conspec. This information would need to be sufficiently precise to allow the range of Japanese macaques to be distinguished from all the other species to be found in the community. Without this, the infant could attach to the wrong species.

Nature–Nurture and the Status of Primal

We hope it is clear to the reader that, with respect to faces, our position is neither strictly nativist nor strictly empiricist. While we argued that the new-born human infant possesses *primal* information concerning the structural characteristics of faces, we are happy to concede that the vast majority of face processing in the adult is performed by a system largely configured by experience of this class of stimuli. Furthermore we reiterate that our notion of *primal* is very different from the commonly used term, 'innate', which is often equated with 'genetic'. We have found that defining *primal* with respect to levels of environmental influence has helped to clarify a number of problems. One example is the age of onset of an ability in question. Sometimes it is suggested that 'innate' can be defined as anything present at the time of birth. One only has to consider puberty to realize the problems with this approach. Within our framework, *primal* abilities can emerge at any point of the life span. Such abilities are not solely genetically determined and the nature of the environmental factors that could give rise to their onset remain to be explored. The normal developmental system (incorporating the species-typical environment) is at least as interesting a topic of study as the effects of the individual-specific environment. Cognitive development should certainly be concerned with both.

There are two issues with regard to a perceptual or cognitive system being *primal*. The first is that the system should be the result of interactions up to and including the non-specific aspects of the species-typical environment. The second is the *level* at which the system is *primal*. For example, we have described how a chick prefers to approach a stuffed hen over many other objects, and how this preference arises without any prior visual experience. While this preference is clearly a primal one, it could have been primal preference for complex visual patterns or the colour orange etc. Only after a series of experiments ruled out these and other alternatives were we able to say that there was a primal preference for the head and neck region.

For a perceptual skill such as face recognition, one has to push the case for lower order psychophysical variables as far as possible. A series of excellent studies by Kleiner and Banks had already pushed the lower level 'sensory hypothesis' for infant face preferences. By re-examining their data we were able to establish that even the most sophisticated form of the sensory hypothesis is unable to account for neonate face preferences. We think, then, that the case for a *primal* Conspec in the human infant, as opposed to a primal, unidimensional sensory preference, has been made.

What options remain to the persistent empiricist? We are both familiar with the claim that 'all' that the new-born infant is interested in is an oval shape with three dots inside, the upper two of which have semi-circles above them. We expect to continue to encounter such claims. But to account for a specific preference for faces in terms of low level sensory dimensions could well lead one into the position of requiring some amazing coincidences. An illustration of this point is made in box 6.1.

In earlier chapters we contrasted a sensory hypothesis, the linear systems model (LSM) with our own, Conspec-based structural hypothesis. In the course of illustrating the difference between the hypotheses we went well beyond the scope of any extant sensory hypotheses, which usually focus only on a single psychophysical dimension. LSM, for example, focuses solely on the amount of energy in a stimulus in the visible part of the spatial frequency spectrum. Our humorous extension of the sensory hypothesis in box 6.1 is obviously an extreme characterization of the sensory hypothesis of face recognition. However, it does have its serious side too. Suppose it were the case that the new-born infant responded to any stimulus as a function of all the sensory factors listed in box 6.1 and that the response to the face were simply the sum of the responses to all the separate dimensions. What conclusion would one then draw? The fact that the human face at optimal distance fitted *all* the dimensions could obviously not be ignored. One option would be to regard it as a remarkable (and highly convenient) coincidence. If this option were rejected then we would have to think in terms of evolutionary explanations. There are two of these. The less likely option would seem to be that the human face has evolved to fit the infant visual system. The other option would be that the human visual system has evolved in such a way that new-born

Box 6.1   The ultimate sensory theory of face preference

The human infant appears to have a preference for faces. How plausible, then, is the idea of sensory-based preference? We have established that accounts based on spatial frequency alone will not serve. There does not appear to be any other single sensory principle which would pick out faces in preference to the various control stimuli used. To make the sensory hypothesis work, then, we would have to use a number of separate principles. Such a story might run something like this:

1 There is a preference for objects projecting an angle of about 6 degrees at the retina – roughly 20 cm. at 1/2 metre.
2 Within objects there is a preference for stimuli with energy at 0.25 cycles/degree in the horizontal plane and 0.5 cycles/degree in the vertical plane.
3 New-borns have a preference for symmetrical stimuli.
      The ideal stimulus would thus be:

4 There is a preference for stimuli without patterning close to the edge.
      The ideal stimulus would be:

5 Stimuli are preferred where the patterning is on the upper half.
      The ideal stimulus would now be:

6 There is a bias towards stimuli with a strong vertical component.
      The ideal stimulus would now be:

7 Stimuli with rounded contours are preferred to those with straight edges.
      The perfect stimulus is:

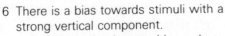

By an astonishing coincidence, the perfect stimulus looks just like a human face.

Note that only a few of the 'principles' used above are actually based on experimental findings. Our intention is to illustrate the complexity of a 'sensory' description of a configural stimulus.

infants are sensitive at points on sensory dimensions such that the face is optimally attractive. Under these hypothetical circumstances, we would still claim that the human infant had a *primal* predisposition to attend to faces. However, this *primal* predisposition would not be a Conspec, since our definition of Conspec requires structural information to be specified.

The position we have just outlined contrasts with the one we would have taken had the LSM story been correct. If faces had been attractive simply because they tended to be visible (compared with a varied collection of control stimuli), then we would not have wanted to claim a *primal* predisposition to attend to faces but only a primal predisposition for that sensory dimension.

The Neuroanatomical Substrate of Conspec and Conlern

The second way that we argued that information from biology could influence our thinking about cognitive development was with regard to the postnatal maturation of the brain. Specifically, we argued that while Conspec is primarily subcortically mediated, Conlern is primarily cortically mediated. In this section we reconsider the evidence from the neural basis of visual attention discussed in chapter three, and attempt to apply it in more detail to Conspec and Conlern.

It is clear that the cortex is already functional to some extent in the new-born.[5] But, as things stand, there is no need to assume that the new-born's preferential orienting toward faces is dependent upon this functioning. Since structures on the retino-collicular (subcortical) circuit are probably capable of responding to species-specific information,[6] and are thought to be involved in orienting to stimuli in the peripheral visual field, it seems highly plausible that they could also mediate the information processing required for the new-born's preferential tracking of faces. If there is any cortical involvement in this new-born behaviour, then the first candidate circuit would be the inhibitory pathway discussed in chapter three, and shown in figure 3.13. The testing methods likely to be particularly sensitive to the functioning of this circuit are habituation and infant control. Since no face preferences are found with these methods in the new-born we believe this form of cortical involvement to be unlikely.[7]

Turning to Conlern, we discussed some evidence in chapter five that favoured the idea of two types of Conlern in the human infant. One of these is an 'averaging', invariance extraction type of Conlern that we called the *similarity* Conlern. This would end up with a representation of the form of an averaged human face.[8] The other Conlern, the *difference* Conlern, is a variance extraction device concerned with encoding the differences between exemplars within a class. This Conlern is concerned with building up detailed representations of individual familiar people. Although these two devices could be linked functionally and anatomically, there is some evidence to suggest that they might be dissociable anatomically. Now, as we have already indicated, discriminating faces from other stimuli would be carried out by the *similarity* Conlern, while recognizing individual familiar faces would be the function of the *difference* Conlern. It has been claimed that stroke patients who are suffering from prosopagnosia, the inability to recognize previously familiar faces, are always capable of distinguishing faces from other stimuli.[9] This suggests that the two kinds of Conlern may indeed be dissociable in terms of their neural basis.[10]

Given that the two mechanisms may be neurally dissociable, a further question concerns which of the neural pathways discussed earlier underlie these mechanisms? One candidate is the inhibitory pathway described in chapter three (p. 75) which is weakly present in the new-born and matures to gain increasing control over the infant's behaviour around one month of age. The developmental timing of this pathway makes it a candidate substrate for the first type of Conlern – the type which, in spite of being the similarity kind, may underlie 'recognition' of mother during the first few days of life. What the *similarity* Conlern knows, the archetypal human face, at this stage will normally be mother's face, since this is the face to which the infant has been predominantly exposed. If the inhibitory pathway is indeed the neural substrate underlying the *similarity* Conlern, then we can actually predict which testing procedures will give rise to a preference for mother's face in the new-born. Let us take as an example the testing procedure used by Bushnell.[11] In this task the new-born infant is moved upright to face toward the blank space between the mother and a stranger's face. Since the infant is quite close to the screen the faces will be far apart. Under these conditions, one or both of the faces will impinge on the peripheral visual field of the infant. Conspec will then cause the infant to orient toward one of the faces. Once the infant is attending to a face, the inhibitory circuit will temporarily (and weakly) inhibit the activity of the colliculus, which reduces the chance that the infant will orient toward other stimuli impinging on the peripheral

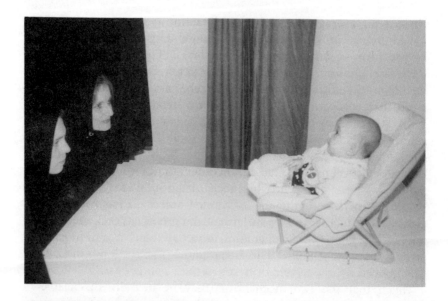

Figure 6.1 *An infant in our replication of the recognition of mother experiment. Infants are presented with the face of their mother and that of a stranger. The amount of time that the infant spends looking at each is recorded. In the top picture the mother and stranger are presented without their hair and face outline.*

visual field. This inhibition will be a little stronger when the infant has its mother's face in foveal vision, rather than a strange face since mother's face will provide a better match to this primitive Conlern.[12] Thus, an infant will more rapidly switch fixation from looking at stranger to looking at mother, than vice versa (figure 6.1).[13]

There is, however, a problem with this account. While Conspec gives rise to a face preference with peripheral stimuli, why doesn't the primitive Conlern mechanism give rise to a face preference with foveal stimuli? The available evidence suggests that over the first few days of life, a new-born learns only the external characteristics of mother's face; probably the face outline and hair shape.[14] This reflects the way the young infant's attention is distributed over the face as indicated by eye fixations.[15] The facial features that the infant has picked up would not be sufficient to discriminate a pattern based on the central features of a face from the scrambled or degraded stimuli used in the typical experiment. The change in scanning patterns required for the infant to learn about the central features of the face do not occur until two months.

What about the second type of Conlern mechanism, the *difference* Conlern? We noted earlier that, in procedures involving foveal presentation, preference for a face pattern starts to appear at about two months of age. We equate this kind of preference with the onset of cortical control through Conlern. This mechanism will correspond to what Scania de Schonen[16] calls the *physiognomy* processor. The time of onset of this preference corresponds with the age when the MT (medial temporal) pathway becomes functional.[17] It therefore seems possible that the second Conlern influences behaviour through this pathway. The subsequent maturation of the frontal eye field pathway may strengthen the influence of these face representations, allowing infants the capacity to 'search' their environment for particular faces.

What is 'Special' about Faces?

Our initial review of the evidence pertaining to infant responses to faces revealed an apparent paradox. New-born infants and two-month-olds preferentially responded to faces, yet one-month-olds did not. This kind of U-shaped performance could not be accounted for by existing theoretical accounts which postulate a single mechanism and led us to a cognitive theory based on biological as well as psychological evidence. Consideration of evidence from other species, and from the postnatal maturation of the brain, led us to propose two mechanisms, Conspec and Conlern. These mechanisms are defined in terms of their functions and were meant to have quite general application. Conspec is a mechanism containing *primal* structural information about the sensory characteristics of a species. In general we discuss the visual features of a species, such as the face, and unless we say otherwise, references to Conspec should be assumed to be visual. But there are many species where we assume that an auditory or olfactory Conspec may be important.

In the human and the chick, the two species we have studied extensively, Conspec contains structural information pertaining to the face of the species. The effect of Conspec in humans is to make it seem that the infant has a preference for faces from birth. Conspec does this by influencing behaviour such that infants will preferentially orient towards any faces that appear in their peripheral visual field. In contrast, with tasks where the stimulus appears in a static location within the central visual field, Conspec will not exert any influence on behaviour. There are other influences on the infant's visual attention, but up to the second month of life Conspec ensures that faces get considerably more exposure than other naturally occurring stimuli. This enables developing cortical circuits to acquire information about faces and, by two months of age infants can discriminate and show preference for faces presented within the central visual field. We gave the name Conlern to the class of mechanisms which acquire information about faces.

This pair of mechanisms in the human infant parallels a pair of mechanisms devoted to mother recognition in the chick. In the chick it has been established that Conspec and Conlern have dissociable neural substrates. We do not wish to make claims about exact homologies between brain structures in the chick and those in the human. Nevertheless, both species share the same basic vertebrate brain design[18] and so it is reasonable to assume that there will be some generalities, at least in the interaction between 'cortical' and 'sub-cortical' pathways. With these considerations in mind, it seemed to us to be worthwhile to speculate on how Conspec and Conlern might be reflected anatomically in the developing human brain. We proposed that over the first two months of life cortical circuits, which are rapidly maturing, configure themselves in a way which reflects their input. As indicated, Conspec guarantees that the infant pays a lot of attention to faces, which results in the acquisition of information about faces by the cortical circuits that underlie Conlern. Some time in the second or third month of life these cortical circuits begin to control the infant's visual attention and, in so doing, inhibit the largely subcortically mediated Conspec. As a result of this, the tasks in which the stimuli appear in the periphery no longer show advantages for faces. In addition, around the age of six weeks there is still no advantage for face stimuli in experiments involving static presentation of stimuli within the central visual field. This may be because the cortex has still not acquired enough information about faces to show such a preference.[19] By two months of age, however, Conlern causes the infant to attend preferentially to faces presented in a static location within the central visual field.

Faces are special, then, for the new-born and the one-month-old in the sense that there is a *primal* mechanism, Conspec, which makes sure that when faces appear outside the central visual field, they are preferentially oriented toward. That is all this mechanism does. It should be clear that we believe that young infants orient to faces under the guidance of a sensory motor reflex; the new-born does not require to understand the 'meaning' of a face. That is to say, there is nothing social or intentional in the new-born's preferential orienting toward faces.

The claim that Conspec is the only 'special' aspect of faces may seem strange since it is clear that the ability of human adults to process faces is outstanding compared with other stimuli.[20] In addition, faces seem to be represented consistently in a relatively small area of the cortex.[21] However, we wish to account for such factors in terms of the interaction between the infant and its environment. Given a normal species-typical environment, regular exposure to a variety of faces is guaranteed. As we have stressed, Conspec will orient the infant's gaze towards these faces. This will ensure that particular cortical circuits, in the process of maturing, and so maximally plastic, are preferentially exposed to faces. For the present we assume that this extensive exposure, combined with constraints arising from the internal cyto-architectonics of the cortex, are sufficient to give rise to cortical circuits specialized for processing faces. That is, we see no need at this stage to assume that there is any face-specific information at birth within these circuits. Such *primal*, face-specific information need only be present in other circuits which we suppose to be primarily subcortical.

Similar arguments apply when we consider the relation between

Conspec and Conlern. Conspec contains information concerning the characteristics of the human face. It would be reasonable to suppose that this information, if not already present in Conlern, should be made available to it somehow. Another reasonable option we have considered is that Conspec acts as a filter, allowing only certain stimuli to get through to Conlern. Either of these possibilities would have the effect of increasing the speed and efficiency of learning about faces in Conlern. However, we have found no evidence to suggest that the human Conspec has any direct relation with Conlern. It would be sufficient that the activity of Conspec preferentially orients the infant toward faces. Note that such an arrangement would not be of much use were it not that the species-typical environment of the child is also favourable for learning about faces. In most cultures, the caretakers of young infants present their faces within viewable distance at frequent intervals. This allows Conspec to shift attention which, in turn, allows Conlern to acquire the appropriate information. Thus it is that while there need be no genetic information to specify faceness within Conlern, and while there is no *primal* specification of Conlern, we can see that if we take a slightly broader biological perspective, that of the species-typical environment, the human Conlern is, in some sense, special.

The equivalent argument applies to the chick. If Conspec had constrained which stimuli would be let through to Conlern, chicks would only have been able to learn the characteristics of objects which satisfied these restrictions. This set would, of course, include hens. However, chicks can acquire information about red boxes or coloured balls. Since such things cannot be specified in the chick's Conspec, we can conclude that there are no internal constraints in the chick's brain from Conspec to the area of the chick's forebrain called IMHV, the site of the chick's Conlern. However, as with the human case, the species-typical environment ensures that 'mother' is normally learned very quickly.

With respect to human development, these general views echo those of Scania de Schonen from the CNRS (Centre Nationale de Recherche Scientifique) in Marseilles. Her theory was put forward most recently in an article written with her colleague Eric Mathivet. Here is their summary.

In adults, as in infants, the right hemisphere is known to process and recognise physiognomies[22] more efficiently than the left hemisphere.

These functions are controlled by neuronal networks, the crucial parts of which have been located in a cortical region which can be defined in humans and non human primates and apparently also in other mammalian species. The multi-modal nature of this region of visual dominance along with the consistency of the contextual perceptual events occurring in the infant's environment might explain why some neuronal networks of this region become specialized in physiognomy processing. The maturational rate of this region in the right hemisphere might be assumed to be faster than that of its left counterpart. This difference in maturational rate together with the absence of inter-hemispheric transfer of information about physiognomy during the first few months of life, along with the limitation of visual sensitivity of infants during this same period of development, suggests that the specialization of this right hemisphere territory in the control of physiognomy processing and recognition might be organized very differently from what happens later on in the left hemisphere as described by authors working on adults.

We do not wish to enter the debate on the exact mechanisms that give rise to lateralization effects in adult face processing.[23] But we are broadly sympathetic to de Schonen and Mathivet's view that the hemisphere in which the processing of individual faces primarily takes place (Conlern) may be determined by a variety of constraining influences, rather than any specifically 'hard-wired' circuits.

De Schonen and Mathivet also suggest that the available evidence from infants and adults supports the idea that there are separate devices for representing faceness on the one hand, and physiognomies on the other. Furthermore, since the faceness detector does not seem to be lateralized, and because of the evidence for its presence shortly after birth, they also speculate that the faceness detector (equivalent to Conspec within our framework) may be subcortically mediated.

Our view, then, is that faces are only special because the infant is born with some structural information about the general characteristics of faces in a primitive pathway concerned with the control of orienting. This information, however, in conjunction with general constraints from cortical cytoarchitectonics and the species-typical environment, is sufficient to 'kick start' a process that results in the highly specialized cortical processing of information in individual faces that we see in the adult. According to this view, cortical specialization for faces is the result of a variety of factors. For example, all faces resemble each other in many respects and differ only in what Diamond and Carey (1986) call 'second-order relationships'; faces belong to members of our own species and therefore have to be categorized and associated with a variety of other visual (body type and gait) and auditory (especially speech) stimuli, and so on. These various interacting factors ensure that faces will tend to be processed in particular parts of the brain. This would lead to a fairly consistent 'localization of function' for face processing, but this is a localization that is created afresh for each individual brain in its interaction with the environment rather than either being specified by genes or being *primal*.

The view we have just put forward contrasts strongly with preformist proposals which would attribute localization entirely to endogenous factors. An extreme example of this contrasting view would be that there is a genetic code which specifies the form of, say, the superior temporal sulcus (STS) in the right hemisphere and the connections of this structure to other structures in the brain such that it is dedicated to the processing of faces and that only faces can be processed there. Such a view would mean that if the STS were damaged at birth then the individual would be destined to be prosopagnosic.[24] Equally, if the individual was blind, STS would not be used for any other function. In contrast, our position predicts that, in the absence of exposure to faces, STS, or whatever other region underlies face recognition in the human adult would subserve some other function. Some support for this prediction has been found in a series of event-related scalp potential studies with congenitally deaf subjects. In these subjects it has been found that cortical regions normally dedicated to higher order auditory analysis appear instead, in the absence of stimulation from the auditory system, to be dedicated to visual analysis.[25] In the same spirit, we surmise that were STS alone to be damaged from birth, not all (and perhaps nothing) of the individual's ability with faces as an adult would be lost. The confluence of information from the various factors associated with faces would result in a different anatomical area becoming specialized in the functions normally carried out in STS. We presume that something of this sort occurs when the language functions appear in the right hemisphere of children with left hemispherectomies.[26] Note that the existence of single cortical cells devoted to particular aspects of face processing cannot be used as evidence for the 'specialness' of faces. The factors already described which lead to the localization of face processing would be sufficient to produce the phenomenon.[27] However, if such cells were to be found at birth, or in the absence of any appropriate specific visual experience then there might be a stronger case for their 'special' status. At the moment, however, such evidence is not forthcoming.[28]

If the *innate* version of STS specialization fails, what of the *primal* version? Our definition of *'primal'* would allow the interaction of the genotype with the internal environment together with non-specific species-typical external environment. In this way, 'special' structures could develop over time without requiring specific inputs. However, as indicated by de Schonen and Mathivet,[29] this specialization does require extensive, specific visual input of faces. This is guaranteed by Conspec, the attention mechanism already in place. It turns out that given the *primal* Conspec, we do not need a *primal* Conlern.[30]

Biology and Cognitive Development

During the project described in this book, spanning some five years of studying infants (and eight years of studying chicks), we have been able to bring together concepts from a variety of disciplines. This has given us new and powerful accounts of the development of cognitive mechanisms. We can see some clear principles emerging with regard to importing biological information into the study of cognitive development. As an example, there are a range of cognitive mechanisms that cannot be studied properly in isolation of the external environment within which they evolve. Hence the somewhat limited usefulness of metaphors derived from computer architectures, since computers have been designed with little reference to and less adaptability to the external environment. The types of cognitive systems that result from our analysis reflect the broader context. Conspec, for example, is a system designed to orient sensory organs for the benefit of other systems. It is only effective within the normal species-typical environment. In an abnormal environment, such as that provided for Egbert (box 3.5), Conspec was not functional because there was nothing around to trigger it. Our view of the purely cognitive construct Conspec in the human infant, then, has been strongly influenced by considerations of neural circuitry in another species, and is only comprehensible in the context of an ethological construct, the species-typical environment.

The next point reveals a difference between cognitive science and biological science. It is that considerations of computational efficiency may simply not be appropriate for understanding the functioning of brains. Cognitive scientists have a tendency to postulate cognitive architectures in which information processing is performed as efficiently as possible. We can demonstrate this with regard to the nature of the interaction between Conspec and Conlern discussed in chapter four. Our informal enquiries have revealed that most psychologists have a strong bias in favour of the form of interaction where Conspec sends a functional 'learn now' signal to Conlern. As we discussed, the evidence in the chick favours the interpretation that there is NO internal interaction between the two systems. The redundancy found in natural systems is easy to underestimate.

A further role for biology is that it gives the cognitive psychologist new dimensions with which to dissociate systems from each other. One of the principle techniques used in describing the functional architecture of the mind is to look for modular construction. Systems may be dissociated from each other on grounds of incompatible or inaccessible information processing. By adopting a biological perspective as well, systems might also be dissociated on grounds of their neural pathways and levels of environmental influence. It is, as yet, a matter of faith rather than necessity that systems dissociated by virtue of neural circuitry will also dissociate with regard to levels of environmental influence, information-processing function and so on. We are encouraged, however, that mother nature seems to be rather cooperative in this respect so far as early abilities are concerned. With many higher cognitive functions in adults, however, the nature of the mapping between function and structure remains unclear.[31]

It is evident that the general framework we have used to explore the development of face recognition could also be applied to other domains such as language acquisition. Traditionally, views of language acquisition have varied from belief in a prespecified 'language organ' to the belief that many apparently universal aspects of language are inevitable given the problem space. The framework we have employed would shift the focus of attention away from this dichotomy toward a discussion of how mechanisms similar to Conspec might interact with the species-typical environment to yield a *primal* substrate for language. A further set of questions would be concerned with the mechanism of interaction of these *primal* structures with the individual-specific aspects of the child's environment, resulting in the acquisition of one language rather than another. Having said this, it was no accident that we chose to focus on the example of face recognition, for this was an area in which there was a substantive body of evidence relating to this ability in other species and other evidence relating to its neural basis. Although researchers in language acquisition may not be quite so fortunate in this regard, we are sufficiently encouraged by recent developments to hope that a similar analysis for this and other domains will not be long in appearing.

We have come to the conclusion that cognitive processes can only be fully appreciated in a biological context. Though most of this book has been concerned with the development of face recognition, we hope that we have said enough to convince the reader that the conclusions we have drawn are general to many aspects of cognitive development. Adjacent branches of science can do more than provide a source of analogy for each other, they can add a level of explanation and provide constraints that result in a clarity missing within the single discipline. We have found that cognitive development can benefit from biology, namely brain development and ethology, in particular ways. We also believe that these aspects of biology need cognition, but that is a topic for another book.

Notes

Chapter 1 Why bring Biology into Cognitive Development?

1 This strong constraint depends crucially on our defining condition 'solely dependent'. To the extent that the change under study required specific environmental input, a psychological account of the change would be needed.

2 Churchland (1986).

3 Fodor (1983).

4 Karmiloff-Smith (1984).

5 We note that cognitive psychology is not alone in its need for metaphors. Indeed, it is difficult to think of any science with a theoretical content, with the possible exception of pure mathematics, that does not depend heavily on metaphors.

6 See, for example, A. Diamond (1988).

7 This point is argued in more detail in Mehler, Morton and Juszyck (1984).

8 We use the term 'biological' in its most general sense – in this case to refer to neuroscience and ethology.

9 Gottlieb (1965; 1979; 1981).

10 Hyland (1984).

11 Oyama (1985). While we are aware that many other authors have espoused similar views (e.g., Johnston (1988)), for the purposes of exposition we focus on one only.

12 Oyama, p. 13.

13 Fodor (1980).

14 See Oyama (1985) chapter 7, fn. 4.

15 See review of Oyama's book by Johnson (1989) for the problems with Oyama's own proposals.

16   It has recently come to our attention that a similar dissociation has been proposed at the neural level by Greenough, Black and Wallace (1987). These authors classify the effects of experience on neural development into 'experience-expectant' (STE in our terms) and 'experience-dependent' (ISE in our terms) components.

17   Within the framework proposed, we define 'genetic' to refer to the interaction at the level of the internal environment.

18   We should note here that we do not expect the notion of a STE to be without its problems as we analyse it in more detail in the future. One can imagine the STE to represent the invariable aspects of the external environment at the time of evolutionary selection. For example, certain human genes were selected for under environmental conditions where water was available on a daily basis. In contrast, some camel genes were selected for under conditions of scarce water supply.

19   This includes sign language.

20   Carmichael (1926).

21   Cruze (1935).

22   Dennis (1940).

23   Dennis and Dennis (1935).

24   Gesell and Thompson (1934).

25   Johnson (1988a); Johnson and Karmiloff-Smith, in press.

26   Excellent introductions to neural development may be found in Hopkins and Brown (1984) and Purves and Lichtman (1985).

27   Ebbesson (1984).

28   See Johnson and Karmiloff-Smith, (in press) for qualifications to this statement.

29   Johnson (1988a).

30   Fodor (1983).

31   Leslie (1988).

32   Karmiloff-Smith (1986).

33   Karmiloff-Smith, *et al.* (in press).

34   J. S. Johnson and E. L. Newport (1989).

35   Johnson and Karmiloff-Smith (in press).

Chapter 2   The Development of Face Recognition

1   Diamond and Carey (1986).

2   We note that while the individual dogs used as stimuli were

champions, none of them had been judged by, or was familiar to, any of the human judges (Carey, personal communication (1990)).

3   Carey and Diamond (1980); Carey, Diamond and Woods (1980).
4   Souther and Banks (1979).
5   Bushnell (1979); Bushnell, Gerry and Burt (1983); Maurer and Salapatek (1976).
6   Maurer and Barrera (1981).
7   Haaf (1974), (1977); Haaf, Smith and Smitty (1983).
8   Gibson (1968), p. 356.
9   Goren, Sarty, and Wu (1975).
10 One reason for this is that the paper was published in a journal not often read by psychologists, and another is that the data presented such a severe challenge to the current views.
11 Maurer and Young attempted to replicate the results reported by Goren *et al.*, and found preferential tracking of the face-like pattern when they used eye movements as the dependent measure. They failed to replicate the preferential head turning observed in the original study however. This failure can be accounted for in terms of the details of the procedure used (see later).
12 Hadyn Ellis is now at the University of Wales, Cardiff.
13 See Johnson *et al.* (1991) for details of procedures.
14 The experimenter's face was too far away from the new-born to see it clearly. Moreover, the experimenters angled their face upward so only the chin and nostrils would be visible.
15 Maurer and Barrera (1981).
16 Maurer (1985).
17 To our knowledge, only one other study has used an infant-control preference procedure around this latter age. This was an earlier study by Robert Fantz who found no advantage for a schematic face over an asymmetrical scrambled face with infants aged from four to six months.
18 Johnson, M.H., *et al.* (in press).
19 Maurer and Barrera (1981).

Chapter 3   Bringing in Biology

1   There are, of course, some exceptions to this general statement. For example, Neisser's (1982) foray into ecological studies of memory.

2   For an overview of the behaviour of the cuckoo see Boswall (1986).

3   Carel Ten Cate (1984).

4   Ten Cate (1989).

5   Wu *et al.* (1980).

6   Fredrickson and Sackett (1984).

7   Sackett and Ruppenthal (1974).

8   There is an assumption here that raising a pigtail macaque in the presence of both rhesus and other pigtail infants leads to equal experience of both. In fact, there is the possibility that pigtail infants behave in a particular way that makes other pigtail infants pay attention to them selectively. This could be a special call for example. The same could be true for stumptail infants with respect to other stumptails. If this were the case, then we could not conclude that the visual preference was *primal*. Instead, we would conclude that the preference for the specific behaviour was *primal*.

9   Swartz (1983).

10   David Perrett, personal communication.

11   Steve Holman, personal communication.

12   Perrett, Rolls and Caan (1982); Bruce *et al.* (1981).

13   Rodman and Gross (1989).

14   Rakic *et al.* 1987.

15   Kendrick and Baldwin (1987).

16   Spalding (1873); Heinroth (1911); Lorenz (1937); Bateson (1966).

17   Cajal (1911); Hebb (1949).

18   Bateson, Horn and Rose (1972).

19   Horn, Rose and Bateson (1973).

20   Bateson, Horn and Rose (1975).

21   See Horn (1985) for a more detailed account of these and subsequent studies.

22   Horn, McCabe and Bateson (1979). The nomenclature of IMHV rather than MHV was introduced in Horn (1981).

23   Kohsaka *et al.* (1979); Maier and Scheich (1983).

24   McCabe *et al.* (1981); (1982).

25   The stimulus used was actually a stuffed jungle fowl, an ancestor of the domestic chicken. For the sake of clear exposition, however, we shall refer to it as a stuffed hen.

26   Horn and McCabe (1984).

27   Bolhuis, McCabe and Horn (1986).

28 Davies *et al.* (1983).
29 DSP4 is a noradrenergic neurotoxin.
30 Davies *et al.* (1985).
31 Coincidentally, the Eagle is the pub where Watson and Crick regularly debated the structure of DNA, and has no doubt been the scene of many a lesser known scientific breakthrough due to its promixity to the Cambridge University laboratories.
32 Hinde (1961).
33 Johnson, *et al.* (1985).
34 Bateson and Wainwright (1972) devised a simultaneous presentation test which is thought to be more sensitive than the sequential test used in the studies discussed so far (see Horn (1985); Johnson and Horn (1987)).
35 See Sluckin (1972), Johnson and Bolhuis (1991) for reviews.
36 For example, see Hinde (1961).
37 Kruhlich, *et al.* (1974).
38 Johnson, *et al.* (1985).
39 Johnson, *et al.* (1989).
40 It has been suggested that non-specific input, such as motor experience, may elevate testosterone levels in the chick brain, which in turn may trigger the predisposition. If this is the case then this putative surge of testosterone has to occur within a particular time window for the 'validation' of the system supporting the predisposition to occur.
41 Dutch (1969); Berryman *et al.* (1971).
42 Banks and Ginsburg (1985).
43 Johnson and Horn (1988).
44 Candland (1969).
45 Domjan and Nash (1988).
46 Johnson and Horn (1988).
47 Johnson and Horn (1986).
48 Johnson and Horn (1987).
49 Johnson and Horn (1987).
50 Bolhuis and Trooster (1988).
51 For example, see Maurer and Lewis (1979); Shephard (1983).
52 Bronson (1974).
53 Similar general arguments have been put forward by Maurer and Lewis (1979) and Atkinson (1984).
54 For example, Slater *et al.* (1988); Bushnell *et al.* (1989).

55 See, for example, Van Essen (1985); de Yoe and Van Essen (1988).
56 For example, Maurer and Lewis (1979); Posner and Rothbart (1980); Atkinson *et al.* (1988).
57 Johnson (1990 a, b).
58 Schiller (1985).
59 See, for example, Johnson (1990a); Marin-Padilla (1990); Rabino-wicz (1979); Conel (1939–67).
60 Aslin (1981).
61 Haith, *et al.* (1988).
62 Robinson, McCarty and Haith (1988).
63 Johnson (1990a) argues that the 'externality effect' and the new-born's increased sensitivity to temporal visual field input an be accounted for by a similar 'collicular' mechanism.

Chapter 4   Conspec, Conlern and the Development of Face Recognition

1 Kleiner and Banks (1987); for quotations see page 594.
2 Note that most of the experiments that have been carried out within this framework have used infants of two months or more. It is tacitly assumed that infants around this age will not have had any prior opportunity to learn about the characteristics of the stimuli being used. Any preferences must, then, reflect more general properties of the visual system. Thus, the underlying philosophy of this work is like that of the new-born studies in trying to understand the nature of inborn abilities.
3 Karmel (1974); Karmel, Hoffman and Fegy (1974), for quotation see page 39.
4 Banks and Salapatek (1981).
5 Gayl *et al.* (1983); Banks and Ginsberg (1985).
6 Banks and Stephens (1982); Banks and Salapatek (1981).
7 Banks and Ginsberg (1985).
8 Slater *et al.* (1985).
9 Gayl *et al.* (1983).
10 Bolhuis *et al.* (1985); Horn (1985).
11 Johnson, Davies and Horn (1989).
12 See Horn (1985).

13   Kleiner (1987).
14   Kleiner (1990), in her response to our position, claimed that the advantage of the face over the Af-Pl stimulus only occurred late in the experiment and, therefore, could be attributed to specific learning of the face. Unfortunately for this argument, a re-analysis of Kleiner's data showed that the advantage of the face over Af-Pl was only true at the beginning of the experiment for each infant. We are inclined, then, to put both of these trends down to chance variation. (We are grateful to Dr Kleiner for her help in resolving this matter.)
15   See also Cioni and Castellacci (1990).
16   Reissland (1988).
17   McCabe et al. (1982).
18   Johnson and Horn (1986).
19   Bateson and Reese (1969).
20   Johnson and Horn (1986).
21   Bateson and Reese (1969).
22   Bolhuis and Johnson (1988).
23   Johnson and Horn (1987).
24   See Bateson (ed.) (1983).
25   Bolhuis et al. 1989.
26   Johnson and Horn (1986).
27   Ellis and Young (1989); de Renzi (1989).
28   Kleiner and Banks (1987).
29   Kleiner (1987).
30   Kleiner and Banks (1987), p. 599.
31   Marler (1976).
32   Bolhuis, et al. (1989).
33   Johnson, Bolhuis and Horn, unpublished observations.

Chapter 5   Conspec and Conlern in the Human Infant

1   Johnson et al. (1991), experiment 2.
2   Bronson (1974); Johnson (1990a); Maurer and Lewis (1989).
3   Johnson et al. (1991), experiment 3.
4   Dodwell (1983); Muir, Abraham, Forbes and Harris (1979).
5   A null result of this kind will always be subject to the criticism that the technique was too insensitive. However, we have used this same technique to obtain discriminatory responses between

non-face stimuli (Johnson, Bartrip and Morton, unpublished data).

6   See Banks and Salapatek (1981).

7   Kleiner (1987).

8   Morton, Johnson and Maurer (1990).

9   For method and further discussion see Morton, Bartrip and Johnson, submitted.

10 Atkinson and Braddick (1980), (1981); Atkinson, Braddick and French (1979).

11 The data were scored both by the sum of the maximum turns to the two sides and by the average of the first three turns. The latter measure is one which Maurer and Young (1983) found was more sensitive than the former. Our analysis confirms the conclusions of Maurer and Young in that the comparisons of the means of the first three looks in all cases gives a more significant difference than comparisons of the maximum looks.

12 Johnson et al. (1991) experiment 2.

13 Biringen (1987).

14 Stucki et al. (1987).

15 Ten Cate (1987).

16 Note that father should be preferred over stranger, and mother over father. Also note the prediction that faces similar to mother's may be recognized with a shorter latency in adult life. This may be a reason for the 'other race effect'. Another prediction is that the 'other race effect' should be stronger in adults whose father was away during early childhood.

17 Bushnell et al. (1989).

18 Field et al. (1984).

Chapter 6   Biology, Cognition and Faces

1   If we looked at the evolutionary history of individual species, we would see that they had arrived at the solution of the problem either by the development of a special *primal* structure or by alterations in the infant's social niche which led to a shift in the species-typical Environment.

2   This is the reason that we have resisted using terms such as genspec for a primal specification sufficient only to distinguish the

genus, a suggestion proffered with some enthusiasm by one of our colleagues.

3 We specify 'visual' here because it is also possible that the cuckoo has an auditory Conspec with which it recognizes the cuckoo call, and so identifies potential mates.

4 Cuckoos also sometimes lay eggs which resemble the eggs of certain hosts, though this is not always the case (Boswell, 1986).

5 See, for example, Atkinson (1984).

6 The prominent ascending projections through the thalamus suggest that the visual processing seen in the superior colliculus could involve the form and pattern discriminations usually attributed only to the cerebral cortex. While there is good evidence for this in the cat (e.g. Berlucchi *et al.* 1972), there is only weak evidence for this ability in the primate (e.g. Anderson and Symmes 1969), probably because the appropriate tasks have not been examined (see Wurtz and Albano 1980).

7 Another possibility for cortical involvement in new-borns' face preferences is that the cells in the temporal lobe are sensitive to faces in the adult macaque (see chapter 3). In the macaque, this area of the temporal lobe receives a direct projection from the deeper layers of the primary visual cortex which are, generally speaking, the first to mature. It is possible, therefore, that this projection influences the subcortical mechanisms controlling orienting in the new-born. This suggestion will have to await further studies on the ontogeny of face-specific cells in the macaque and sheep.

8 Eventually it may be fast acting and error prone – the mechanism responsible for us seeing a face in the moon, in clouds or in a snowman. Its function is to alert us to the presence of a possibly unknown person and to activate the process whereby we will be able to interpret the intentions of persons from their facial expression.

9 Benton (1990); de Renzi (1986).

10 It is intriguing to note that patients with Balint's syndrome (dorsal simultaneous agnosia) from bilateral lesions at the parietal occipital junction appear to be unable to track most stimuli except faces. Furthermore, a consistent clinical observation is that patients coming out of coma will track faces long before any other stimuli that have been tested (B. Rafal, Martinez VA, pers. comm. 28 Jan. 1991). These observations suggest that evidence

dissociating Conspec from Conlern may be obtained in adult clinical populations.

11 Described in chapter 5 (p. 00).

12 We note that, in general, the inhibition will also grow stronger over the first month or so of life, resulting in the apparent inability of infants around one month to disengage their gaze from even quite 'dull' stimuli.

13 We note that, by some versions of this account, the new-born will be generally less distractable when mother is within the foveal field. That is, it predicts that any stimulus presented in the peripheral visual field will be less likely to initiate an orientation.

14 Maurer and Salapatek (1976). Note that there are also problems with the functionality of the retina during this period (Abramov, et al., 1982).

15 Maurer and Salapatek (1976).

16 For example, de Schonen and Mathivet (1989).

17 Johnson (1990a).

18 Horn (1985); Macphail (1982).

19 An option is that the cortical circuits, while mature enough to exercise control over the infant's attention, are still not mature enough to exercise control over the infant's behaviour. Here is one case where developmental neuroanatomy could provide the answer. If it could be shown that there were suitable connections from the cortex for the exercise of control, then we could presume that our first suggestion was correct.

20 See Bruce (1988) for a review.

21 Benton (1990, p. 493) says 'the integrity of the right inferior occipitotemporal area, where, conceivably, visual information is being transmitted to the mesial and inferior temporal region on the way to being linked up with a memory store, appears to be a crucial juncture, injury to which leads to an impairment in the recognition of familiar faces.'

22 The characteristics that define an individual face, as opposed to a face-like pattern.

23 de Schonen and Mathivet (1989). But see commentators on the original article.
The issue of whether prosopagnosia in the human adult results from damage to analogous regions to STS, or its inputs or outputs, is a controversial one but does not affect the gist of our argument. See Perrett et al. (1982) for discussion.

25 Neville (1991), Neville and Lawson (1987). In addition, Rauschecker and Harris (1983) and Rice (1979) point to auditory
system reorganisation after blindness.
26 Bishop (1983).
27 See Morton and Johnson (1989).
28 See p. 45, chapter three.
29 de Schonen and Mathivet (1989).
30 The similarity Conlern, on the one hand, is the product of the
interaction between the animal and the SPECIFIC aspects of the
species-typical environment. The difference Conlern is the
product of the interaction between the animal and the individual-
specific environment.
31 Mehler, Morton and Jusczyk (1984); Morton (1984).

References

Abramov, I., Gordon, J., Hendrickson, A., Hainline, L., Dobson, V. and Laboussier, E. (1982). 'The retina of the newborn human infant', *Science*, 217, 265–7.

Anderson, K. V. and Symmes, D. (1969). 'The superior colliculus and higher visual functions in the monkey'. *Brain Research*, 13, 37–52.

Aslin, R. N. (1981). 'Development of smooth pursuit in human infants', in: D. F. Fisher, R. A. Monty and J. W. Senders (eds.), *Eye Movements: Cognition and Visual Perception* Hillsdale, NJ: Erlbaum.

Atkinson, J. (1984). 'Human visual development over the first six months of life: a review and a hypothesis', *Human Neurobiology*, 3, 61–74.

—— and Braddick, O. (1980). 'Assessment of vision in infants: applications to amblyopia', *Transactions of the Ophthalmic Societies of the United Kingdom*, 99, 338–43.

—— and Braddick, O. (1981). 'Acuity, contrast sensitivity and accommodation in infancy', In R. N. Aslin, J. R. Alberts and M. R. Peterson (eds), *Development of Perception: Psychobiological Perspectives: Psychobiological perspectives: Vol. 2, The visual system.* New York: Academic Press.

——, Braddick, O. and French, J. (1979). 'Contrast sensitivity of the human neonate measured by the visually evoked potential', *Investigative Ophthalmology and Visual Science*, 18, 210–13.

——, Hood, B., Wattam-Bell, J., Anker, S. and Tricklebank, J. (1988). 'Development of orientation discrimination in infants', *Perception*, 17, 587–95.

Banks, M. S. and Ginsberg, A. P. (1985). 'Infant visual preferences: a review and new theoretical treatment', in H. W. Reese (ed.),

Advances in child development and behaviour vol. 19, (New York: Academic).

—— and Salapatek, P. (1981). 'Infant pattern vision: A new approach based on the contrast sensitivity function', *Journal of Experimental Child Psychology*, 31, 1–45.

—— and Stephens, B. R. (1982). 'The contrast sensitivity of human infants to gratings differing in duty cycle', *Vision Research*, 22, 739–44.

Bartashunas, C. and Suboski, M. D. (1984). 'Effects of age of chick on social transmission of pecking preferences from hen to chicks', *Developmental Psychobiology*, 17, 121–7.

Bateson, P. P. G. (1966). 'The characteristics and context of imprinting', *Biological Review*, 41, 177–220.

—— (1972). 'The formation of social attachments in young birds', *Proceedings of the XVth International ornithological congress* (Leiden: E. J. Brill).

—— (ed.) (1983). *Mate Choice* (Cambridge: CUP).

——, Horn, G. and Rose, S. P. R. (1972). 'Effects of early experience on regional incorporation of precursors into RNA and protein in the chick brain', *Brain Research*, 39, 449–65.

——, Horn, G. and Rose, S. P. R. (1975). 'Imprinting: correlations between behaviour and incorporation of [14C] uracil into chick brain', *Brain Research*, 84, 207–20.

—— and Reese, E. P. (1969). 'The reinforcing properties of conspicuous stimuli in the imprinting situation', *Animal Behavior*, 17, 629–99.

—— and Wainwright, A. A. P. (1972). 'The effects of prior exposure to light on the imprinting process in domestic chicks', *Behaviour*, 42, 279–90.

Benton, A. (1990). 'Facial recognition 1990', *Cortex*, 26, 491–9.

Berlucchi, G., Sprague, J. M., Levy, J. and DiBerardino, A. C. (1972). 'Pretectum and superior colliculus in visually guided behaviour and in flux and form discrimination in the cat', *Journal of Comparative and Physiological Psychology*, 78, 123–72.

Berryman, J., Fullerton, C. and Sluckin, W. (1971). 'Complexity and colour preferences of chicks of different ages', *Quarterly Journal of Experimental Psychology*, 23, 255–60.

Bever, T. G. (ed.) (1982). *Regressions in Mental Development: Basic Phenomena and Theories* (Hillsdale, NJ: Lawrence Erlbaum).

Biringen, Z. C. (1987). 'Infant attention to facial expressions and facial motion', *Journal of Genetic Psychology*, 148, 127–33.

Bishop, D. V. M. (1983). 'Linguistic impairment after left hemi-decortication for infantile hemiplegia? A reappraisal', *Quarterly Journal of Experimental Psychology*, 35A, 199–208.

Bolhuis, J. J. and Johnson, M. H. (1988). 'Effects of response-contingency and stimulus presentation schedule on imprinting in the chick', *Journal of Comparative Psychology*, 102, 61–5.

——, Johnson, M. H. and Horn, G. (1985). 'Effects of early experience on the development of filial preferences in the domestic chick', *Developmental Psychobiology*, 18, 299–308.

——, Johnson, M. H. and Horn, G. (1989). 'Interacting processes during imprinting: the development of a predisposition does not prevent learning', *Journal of Experimental Psychology: Animal Behaviour Processes*, 15, 376–82.

——, Johnson, M. H., Horn, G. and Bateson, P. (1989). 'Long-lasting effects of IMHV lesions on social preferences in the domestic fowl'. *Behavioral Neuroscience*, 103, 438–41.

——, McCabe, B. J. and Horn, G. (1986). 'Androgens and imprinting. Differential effects of testoserone on filial preferences in the domestic chick', *Behavioral Neuroscience*, 100, 51–6.

—— and Trooster, W. J. (1988). 'Reversibility revisited: stimulus-dependent stability of filial preference in the chick', *Animal Behavior*, 36, 668–74.

Boswall, J. (1986). *Birds For All Seasons* (London: BBC Publications).

Braddick, O. J., Wattam-Bell, J. and Atkinson, J. (1986). 'Orientation-specific cortical responses develop in early infancy', *Nature*, 320, 617–9.

Bronson, G. W. (1974). 'The postnatal growth of visual capacity', *Child Development*, 45, 873–90.

Bruce, C. J., Desimone, R. and Gross, C. G. (1981. 'Visual properties of neurons in a polysensory area in superior temporal sulcus of the macaque', Journal of Neurophysiology, 20, 515–21.

Bruce, V. (1988). *Recognising Faces* (Hove: Lawrence Erlbaum).

Bushnell, I. W. R. (1979). 'Modification of the externality effect in young infants', *Journal of Experimental Child Psychology*, 28, 211–29.

——, Gerry G. and Burt, K. (1983). 'The externality effect in neonates', *Infant Behaviour and Development*, 6, 151–6.

——, Sai, F. and Mullin, J. T. (1989). 'Neonatal recognition of the mother's face', *British Journal of Developmental Psychology*, 7, 3–15.

Cajal, S. R. (1911). *Histologie du System Nerveux de l'Homme et des Vertebres*, vol. 2 (Paris: Maloine).

Candland, D. K. (1969). 'Discrimination of facial regions used by the domestic chick in maintaining the social dominance order', *Journal of Comparative and Physiological Psychology*, 69, 281–5.

Carey, S. and Diamond, R. (1980). 'Maturational determination of the developmental course of face encoding', in *Biological Studies of Mental Processes*, Caplan, D. (ed.), (Cambridge, Mass: MIT Press).

——, Diamond, R. and Woods, B. (1986). 'Developmental of face recognition–a maturational component?', *Developmental Psychology*, 16, 257–69.

Carmichael, L. (1926). 'The development of behavior in invertebrates experimentally removed from the influence of external stimulation', *Psychological Review*, 33, 51–8.

Changeux, J.-P. (1983). *L'Homme Neuronal* (Paris: Fayard).

Cherfas, J. and Scott, A. (1981). 'Impermanent reversal of filial imprinting', *Animal Behavior*, 30, 301.

Churchland, P. S. (1986). *Neurophilosophy* (Cambridge, Mass: MIT/ Bradford Books).

Cioni, G. and Castellaci, A. M. (1990). 'Development of fetal and neonatal motor activity: implications for neurology', in H. Bloch and B. I. Bertenthal (eds), *Sensory Motor Organisation and Development in Infancy and Early Childhood* (Dordrecht: Kluver Academic Publishers).

Conel, J. L. (1939–67). *The Postnatal Development of the Human Cerebral Cortex, Vols. I–VIII* (Cambridge, Mass: Harvard University Press.)

Cruze, W. W. (1935). 'Maturation and learning in chicks', *Journal of Comparative Psychology*, 19, 371–408.

Davies, D. C., Horn, G. and McCabe, B. J. (1983). 'Changes in telencephalic catecholamine levels in the domestic chick: Effects of age and visual experience', *Developmental Brain Research*, 10, 251–5.

——, Horn, G. and McCabe, B. J. (1985). Noradrenaline and learning: the effects of the noradrenergic neurotoxin DSP4 on imprinting in the domestic chick'. *Behavioral Neuroscience*, 99, 652–60.

——, Taylor, D. and Johnson, M. H. (1988). 'Restricted hyperstriatal lesions and passive avoidance learning in the chick', *Journal of Neuroscience*, 8, 4662–8.

de Courten, C. and Garey, L. J. (1982). 'Morphology of the neurones in the human lateral geniculate nucleus and their normal development', *Experimental Brain Research*, 47, 259–71.

Dennis W. (1940). 'The effect of cradling practices upon the onset of walking in Hopi children', *Journal of Genetic Psychology*, 56, 77–86.

—— and Dennis M. (1935). 'The effect of restricted practice upon the reaching, sitting and standing of two infants', *Journal of Genetic Psychology*, 47, 17–32.

de Renzi, E. (1986). 'Current issues on prosopagnosia', in H. D. Ellis, M. A. Jeeves, F. Newcombe and A. Young (eds), *Aspects of Face Processing* (Dordrecht: Nijhoff).

—— (1989). 'Prosopagnosia: a multi-stage, specific disorder?' in A. W. Young and H. D. Ellis, *Handbook of Research on Face Processing* (Amsterdam: North-Holland).

de Schonen, S. and Mathivet, E. (1989). 'First come, first served: a scenario about the development of hemispheric specialization in face recognition in infancy', *European Bulletin of Cognitive Psychology*, 9, 3–45.

de Yoe, E. A. and Van Essen, D. C. (1988). 'Concurrent processing streams in monkey visual cortex', *Trends in Neuroscience*, 11, 219–26.

Diamond, A. (1988). 'Differences between adult and infant cognition: is the crucial variable presence an absence of language?' in L. Weiskrantz (ed.), *Thought without Language* (Oxford: OUP).

—— and Goldman-Rakic, P. S. (1983). 'Comparison of performance on a Piagetian object permanence task in human infants and rhesus monkeys: evidence for involvement of prefrontal cortex', *Neuroscience Abstracts*, 9, 641.

Diamond, R. and Carey, S. (1986). 'Why faces are and are not special: an effect of expertise', *Journal of Experimental Psychology: General*, 115, 107–17.

Dodwell, P. C. (1983). 'Spatial sense of the human infant', in A. Hein and M. Jeannerod (eds), *Spatially Oriented Behavior* (New York: Springer-Verlag).

Domjan, M. and Nash, S. (1988). 'Stimulus control of social behaviour in male Japanese quail', *Animal Behaviour*, 36, 1006–15.

Dutch, J. (1969). 'Visual complexity and stimulus pacing in chicks', *Quarterly Journal of Experimental Psychology*, 64, 281–5.

Ebbesson S. O. E. (1984). 'Evolution and ontogeny of neural circuits', *Behavioral and Brain Sciences*, 7, 321–31.

Ellis, H. D. and Young, A. (1989). 'Are faces special?' In A. W. Young and H. D. Ellis, *Handbook of Research on Face Processing.* (Amsterdam: North-Holland).

Fagg, G. E. and Matus, A. (1984). 'Selective association of N-methyl D-aspartate and quisqualate types of L-glutamate receptor with post-synaptic densities', *Procedings of the National Academy of Science*, 81, 6876–80.

Field, T. M., Cohen, D., Garcia, R. and Greenberg, R. (1984). 'Mother-stranger face discrimination by the newborn', *Infant Behaviour and Development*, 7, 19–25.

Fodor J. (1980). 'Fixation of belief and concept acquisition', in M. Piattelli-Palmarini (ed.), *Language and Learning* (Cambridge, Mass: Harvard University Press).

—— (1983). *Modularity of Mind* (Cambridge, Mass: MIT/Bradford Books).

Fredrickson, W. T. and Sackett, G. T. (1984). *Journal of Comparative Psychology*, 98, 29–34.

Friede, R. L. and Hu, K. H. (1967). 'Proximo-distal differences in myelin development in human optic fibres', *Zeitschrift Zellforsch*, 79, 259–64.

Gayl, I. E., Roberts, J. O. and Werner, J. S. (1983). 'Linear systems analysis of visual pattern preferences', *Journal of Experimental Child Psychology*, 35, 30–45.

Geschwind, N. and Galaburda, A. M. (1985). Cerebral lateralization: Biological mechanisms, associations, and pathology. *Archives of Neurology*, 42, 428–462; 521–56, 634–54.

Gesell A. and Thompson H. (1943). 'Learning and maturation in identical infant twins: an experimental analysis by the method of co-twin control', in Barker, Kounir and Wright, *Child behavior and development* (New York: McGraw-Hill).

Gibson, E. J. (1969) *Principles of perceptual learning and development* (New York: Appleton-Century-Crofts).

Goren, C. C., Sarty, M. and Wu, P. Y. K. (1975). 'Visual following and pattern discrimination of face-like stimuli by newborn infants', *Pediatrics*, 56, 544–9.

Gottlieb, G. (1965b). 'Prenatal auditory sensitivity in chickens and ducks', *Science*, 147, 1596–8.

—— (1979). 'Development of species identification in ducklings,

V. Perceptual differentiation in the embryo', *Journal of Comparative and Physiological Psychology*, 93, 831–54.

—— (1981). 'Roles of early experience in species-specific perceptual development', in Aslin, R. N., Alberts, J. R. and Petersen, M. R. (eds), *Development of Perception, Vol. 1* (New York: Academic Press).

Greenough, W. J. (1986). 'What's special about development? Thoughts on the bases of experience-sensitive synaptic plasticity', in Greenough, W. J. and Juraska, J. M. (eds), *Developmental Neuropsychobiology*. (Academic Press: London).

Greenough, W. T., Black, J. E. and Wallace, C. S. (1987). 'Experience and Brain Development', *Child Development*, 58, 539–59.

Guiton, P. (1959). 'Socialisation and imprinting in brown leghorn chicks'. *Animal Behaviour*, 7, 26–34.

Haaf, R. (1974). 'Complexity and facial resemblance as determinants of response to facelike stimuli by 5- and 10-week-old infants', *Journal of Experimental Child Psychology*, 18, 480–7.

—— (1977). 'Visual response to complex facelike patterns by 15- and 20-week-old infants', *Developmental Psychology*, 13, 77–8.

——, Smith, P. and Smitty, S. (1983). 'Infant responses to facelike patterns under fixed-trial and infant-control procedures', *Child Development*, 54, 172–7.

Haith, M. M., Hazan, C. and Goodman, G. S. (1988). 'Expectation and anticipation of dynamic visual events by 3–5-month old babies', *Child Development*, 59, 467–79.

Hebb, D. O. (1949). *The organization of behaviour* (New York: John Wiley).

Heinroth, O. (1911). 'Beitrage zur Biologie nahmentlich Ethologie und Psychologie der Anatiden'. *Verh. 5th int. orn. kong. Berlin*, 589–702.

Hess, E. H. (1959). 'Imprinting', *Science*, 130, 133–41.

Hinde, R. A.(1961). 'The establishment of parent–offspring relations in birds, with some mammalian analogies', in: W. H. Thorpe and O. L. Zangwill (eds), *Current problems in animal behaviour* (Cambridge: CUP).

Hopkins, W. G. and Brown, M. C. (1984). *Development of nerve cells and their connections*. (Cambridge: CUP).

Horn, G. (1981). 'Neural mechanisms of learning: An analysis of imprinting in the domestic chick', *Proceedings of the Royal Society of London, Series B*, 213, 101–37.

Horn, G. (1985). *Memory, imprinting and the brain*. (Oxford: Clarendon Press).

——, Bradley, P. and McCabe, B. J. (1985). 'Changes in the structure of synapses associated with learning', *Journal of Neuroscience*, 5, 3161–8.

—— and McCabe, B. J. (1984). 'Predispositions and preferences. Effects on imprinting of lesions to the chick brain', *Animal Behaviour*, 32, 288–92.

——, McCabe, B. J. and Bateson, P. P. G. (1979). 'An autoradiographic study of the chick brain after imprinting', *Brain Research*, 168, 361–73.

—— , Rose, S. P. R. and Bateson, P. P. G. (1973). 'Monocular imprinting and regional incorporation of tritiated uracil into the brains of intact and "split-brain" chicks', *Brain Research*, 56, 227–37.

Huttenlocher, P. R., de Courten, C., Garey, L. G. and Van der Loos, H (1982). 'Synaptogenesis in human visual cortex-evidence for synapse elimination during normal development', *Neuroscience Letters*, 33, 247–52.

Hyland M. E. (1984). 'Interactionism and the person x situation debate', in Royce J. R. and Mos L. P. (eds), *Annals of theoretical psychology* vol. 2 (New York: Plenum).

Immelmann, K. (1972). 'Sexual and other long term aspects of imprinting in birds and other species', in D. H. Lehrman, R. A. Hinde and E. Shaw (eds), *Advances in the Study of Behaviour* (New York: Academic Press).

Jaynes, J. (1956). 'Imprinting: the interaction of learned and innate behaviour. I. Development and generalisation', *Journal of Comparative Physiological and Psychology*, 49, 200–6.

Johnson, J. S. and Newport, E. L. (1989). 'Critical period effects in second language learning: the influence of maturational state on the acquisition of English as a second language', *Cognitive Psychology*, 21, 60–99.

Johnson, M.H. (1987). 'Brain maturation and the development of face recognition in early infancy', *Behavioural Brain Research*, 26, 224.

—— (1988a). 'Parcellation and plasticity: implications for ontogeny', *The Behavioural and Brain Sciences*, 11, 547–9.

—— (1988b). 'Memories of mother', *New Scientist*, 1600, 60–2.

—— (1990a). 'Cortical maturation and the development of visual attention in early infancy', *Journal of Cognitive Neuroscience*, 2, 81–95.

—— (1990b). 'Cortical maturation and perceptual development', in H. Block and B. Bertenthal (eds), *Sensory Motor Organisation and Development in Infancy and Early Childhood* (Dordrecht: Kluver Academic Publishers).

—— (1991). 'Information processing and storage during filial imprinting', in P. G. Hepper (ed.), *Kin Recognition*. (Cambridge: CUP).

—— and Bolhuis, J. J. (1991). 'Imprinting, predispositions and filial preference in the chick', in R. J. Andrew (ed.), *Neural and Behavioural Plasticity* (Oxford: OUP).

——, Bolhuis, J. J. and Horn, G. (1985). 'Interaction between acquired preferences and developing predispositions during imprinting', *Animal Behaviour*, 33, 1000–6.

——, Davies, D. C. and Horn, G. (1989). 'A sensitive period for the development of filial preferences in dark-reared chicks', *Animal Behaviour*, 37, 1044–6.

—— , Dziurawiec, S., Bartrip, J. and Morton, J. (in press). 'Infants preferences for face-like stimuli: effects of the movement of internal features', *Infant Behaviour and Development*.

——, Dziurawiec, S., Ellis, H. D. and Morton, J. (1991). 'Newborns preferential tracking of faces and its subsequent decline', *Cognition*, 40, YY–ZZ.

—— and Horn, G. (1986). 'Dissociation of recognition memory and associative learning by a restricted lesion of the chick forebrain', *Neuropsychologia*, 24, 329–40.

—— and Horn, G. (1987). 'The role of a restricted lesion of the chick forebrain in the recognition of individual conspecifics', *Behavioral Brain Research*, 23, 269–75.

—— and Horn, G. (1988). 'Development of filial preferences in dark-reared chicks', *Animal Behavior*, 36, 675–83.

—— and Karmiloff-Smith, A. (in press). 'Can neural selectionism be applied to cognitive development and its disorders', *New Ideas in Psychology*.

Johnston, T.D. (1988). 'Developmental explanation and the ontogeny of birdsong: nature/nurture redux', *Behavioral and Brain Sciences*, 11, 617–63.

Karmel, B. Z. (1974). 'Contour effects and pattern preferences in infants: a reply to Greenberg and O'Donnell (1972)', *Child Development*, 45, 196–9.

——, Hoffmann, R. F. and Fegy, M. J. (1974). 'Processing of contour information by human infants evidenced by pattern-dependent evoked potentials', *Child Development*, 45, 39–48.

Karmiloff-Smith, A. (1984). 'Children's problem solving', In M. E. Lamb, A. L. Brown and B. Rogoff (eds), *Advances in Developmental Psychology, Vol. III* (Hillsdale, N.J.: Erlbaum).

—— (1986). 'From metaprocesses to conscious access: evidence from children's metalinguistic and repair data', *Cognition*, 23, 2, 95–147.

——, Johnson, H., Bartrip, J., Karmiloff, Y-N., Jones, M. C., Grant, J. and Cuckle, P. (in press). 'From sentential to discourse functions: detection and explanation of speech repairs in children and adults'.

Kendrick, K. M. and Baldwin, B. A. (1987). 'Cells in temporal cortex of conscious sheep can respond preferentially to the sight of faces', *Science*, 236, 448–50.

Kleiner, K. A. (1987). 'Amplitude and phase spectra as indices of infant's pattern preferences', *Infant Behaviour and Development*, 10, 49–59.

—— (1990). 'Models of neonates' preferences for facelike patterns: a response to Morton, Johnson and Maurer', *Infant Behaviour and Development*, 13, 105–8

—— and Banks, M. S. (1987). 'Stimulus energy does not account for 2-month-old preferences', *Journal of Experimental Psychology: Human Perception and Performance*, 13, 594–600.

Kohaska, S., Takamatsu, K., Aoki, E. and Tsukada, Y. (1979). 'Metabolic mapping of the chick brain after imprinting using [14C] 2-deoxyglucose technique', *Brain Research*, 172, 539–44.

Kossut, M. and Rose, S. P. R. (1984). 'Differential 2-deoyxglucose uptake into chick brain structures during passive avoidance training', *Neuroscience*, 12, 971–7.

Kruhlich L., Hefco E. and Read C. B. (1974). 'The effect of acute stress on the secretion of LH, FSH, prolactin and GH in the normal rat, with comments on their statistical evaluation', *Neuroendocrinology*, 16, 293–311.

Lee-Teng, E. and Sherman, M. S. (1966). 'Memory consolidation of one-trial learning in chicks', *Proceedings of the National Academy of Science*, 56, 926–31.

Leslie, A. M. (1988). 'The necessity of illusion: perception and thought in infancy', in L. Weiskrantz (ed.), *Thought Without Language* (Oxford: OUP).

Leuba G. and Garey L. J. (1982). 'A morphometric developmental study of dendrites in the lateral geniculate of the monkey', *Neuroscience*, 7 (Suppl.), 131.

—— and Garey, L. J. (1987). 'Evolution of neuronal numerical density in the developing and aging human visual cortex', *Human Neurobiology*, 6, 11–18.

Lickliter, R. and Gottlieb, G. (1986a). 'Training ducklings in broods interferes with maternal imprinting', *Developmental Psychobiology*, 19, 555–66.

—— and Gottlieb, G. (1986b). 'Visually imprinted maternal preference in ducklings is redirected by social interaction with siblings', *Developmental Psychobiology*, 19, 265–77.

—— and Gottlieb, G. (1988). 'Social specificity: interaction with own species is necessary to foster species-specific maternal preference in ducklings', *Developmental Psychobiology*, 21, 311–21.

Lorenz, K. (1937). 'The companion in the bird's world', *Auk*, 54, 245–73.

McCabe, B. J., Cipolla-Neto, J., Horn, G. and Bateson, P. P. G. (1982). 'Amnesic effects of bilateral lesions placed in the hyperstriatum ventrale of the chick after imprinting', *Experimental Brain Research*, 48, 13–21.

—— and Horn, G. (1988). 'Learning and memory: regional changes in N-methyl-D-aspartate receptors in the chick brain', *Proceedings of the National Academy of Science*, 85, 2849–53.

——, Horn, G. and Bateson, P. (1981). 'Effects of restricted lesions of the chick forebrain on the acquisition of preferences during imprinting', *Brain Research*, 205, 29–37.

Macphail, E. M. (1982). *Brain and Intelligence in Vertebrates* (Oxford: Clarendon Press).

Maier, V. and Scheich, H. (1983). 'Acoustic imprinting leads to differential 2-deoxy-D-glucose uptake in the chick forebrain', *Proceedings of the National Academy of Science, USA*, 80, 3860–4.

Mandler, J. M. (1990). 'Preverbal recall of event sequencies', in A. Diamond (ed.), *The Development and Neural Basis of Higher Cognitive Functions* (New York: New York Academy of Sciences Press).

Mann, I. C. (1964). *The Development of the Human Eye* (London: British Medical Association).

Marin-Padilla, M. (1976). 'Pyramidal cell abnormalities in the motor cortex of a child with Down Syndrome', *Journal of Comparative Neurology*, 63–82.

Marin-Padilla, M. (1990). 'The pyramidal cell and its local-circuit interneurones: a hypothetical unit of the mammalian cerebral cortex', *Journal of Cognitive Neuroscience*, 2, 180–94.

Marler, P. (1976). 'Sensory templates in species-specific behaviour', in J. C. Fentress (ed.), *Simpler Networks and Behaviour* (Sunderland, Mass: Sinauer).

Maurer, D. (1985). 'Infants' perception of facedness', in T. N. Field, and N. Fox, (eds), *Social Perception in Infants* (New Jersey: Ablex).

—— and Barrera, M. (1981). 'Infants' perception of natural and distorted arrangements of a schematic face', *Child Development*, 47, 523–7.

—— and Lewis, T. L. (1979). 'A physiological explanation of infants' early visual development', *Canadian Journal of Psychology*, 33, 232–52.

—— and Lewis, T. L. (in press). In M. Weiss and P. Zelazo (eds), *Newborn Attention: Biological Constraints and the Influence of Experience* (Norwood, NJ: Ablex).

—— and Salapatek, (1976). 'Developmental changes in the scanning of faces by young infants', *Child Development*, 47, 523–7.

—— and Young, R. (1983). 'Newborns' following of natural and distorted arrangements of facial features', *Infant Behaviour and Development*, 6, 127–31.

Mehler, J., Morton, J. and Jusczyk P. W. (1984). 'On reducing language to biology', *Cognitive Neuropsychology*, 1, 83–116.

Morton, J. (1984). 'Brain-based and non-brain-based models of language', in D. Caplan, A. R. Lecours and A. Smith (eds), *Biological Perspectives in Language* (Cambridge, Mass: MIT Press).

—— , Bartrip, J. and Johnson, M. H. (submitted). 'Two mechanisms underlie infant responses to face-like and other patterns'.

—— and Johnson, M. H. (1989). 'Four ways for faces to be "special"', in A. W. Young and H. D. Ellis (eds), *Handbook of Research on Face Processing* (Amsterdam: North-Holland).

——, Johnson, M. H. and Maurer, D. (1990). 'On the reasons for newborns' responses to faces', *Infant Behavior and Development*, 13, 99–104.

Muir, D. W., Abraham, W., Forbes, B. and Harris, L. S. (1979). 'The ontogenesis of an auditory localisation reponse from birth of four months of age', *Canadian Journal of Psychology*, 33, 320–33.

Neisser, U. (1976). *Cognition and Reality: Principles and implications of Cognitive Psychology*. (San Francisco: W. H. Freeman).

—— (1982). *Memory Observed* (San Francisco: W. H. Freeman).

Neville, H. (1991). 'Neurobiology of cognitive and language processing: effects of early experience', in K. R. Gibson and A. C. Petersen (eds), *Brain Maturation and Cognitive Development* (Hawthorne, NY: Aldine de Gruyter).

—— and Lawson, D. (1987). 'Attention to central and peripheral visual space in a movement detection task: an event-related potential and behavioral study. II Congenitally deaf adults', *Brain Research*, 405, 268–83.

Oyama, S. (1985). *The ontogeny of information* (Cambridge: CUP).

Patterson, T. A, Alvarado, M. C., Warner, I. T, Bennet, E. L. and Rosenzweig, M. R. (1986). 'Memory stages and brain asymmetry in chick learning', *Behavioral Neuroscience*, 100, 856–65.

Payne, J. K. and Horn, G. (1984). 'Long-term consequences of exposure to an imprinting stimulus on spontaneous impulse activity in the chick brain', *Behavioral Brain Research*, 13, 155–62.

Perrett, D. I., Rolls, E. T. and Caan, W. (1982). 'Visual neurones responsive to faces in the monkey temporal cortex', *Experimental Brain Research*, 47, 329–42.

Posner, M. I. and Rothbart, M. K. (1980). 'The development of attentional mechanisms', in J. H. Flower (ed.), *Nebraska Symposium on Motivation* (Lincoln, Nebraska: University of Nebraska Press).

Purves, D. and Lichtman, J. W. (1985). *Principles of Neural Development* (Sunderland, Mass: Sinaner Associates).

Rabinowicz, T. (1979). 'The differential maturation of the human cerebral cortex', in F. Falkner and J. M. Tanner (eds), *Human Growth, Vol. 3, Neurobiology and Nutrition* (New York: Plenum).

Rakic, P., Bourgeois, J. P., Eckenhoff, M. F., Zecevic, M. and Goldman-Rakic, P. S. (1986). 'Concurrent overproduction of synapses in diverse regions of the primate cerebral cortex', *Science*, 232, 232–5.

Rauschecker, J. P. and Harris, L. (1983). 'Auditory compensation of the effects of visual deprivation in the cat's superior colliculus', *Experimental Brain Research*, 50, 69–83.

Reissland, N. (1988). 'Neonatal imitation in the first hour of life: observations in rural Nepal', *Developmental Psychology*, 24, 464–9.

Rice, C. (1979). 'Early blindness, early experience, and perceptual enhancement', *Research Bulletin, American Foundation for the Blind*, 22, 1–22.

Robinson, N. S., McCarty, M. E. and Haith, M. M. (1988). 'Visual expectations in early infancy', paper presented at the International Conference on Infant Studies, Washington, DC.

Rockland, K. S. and Pandya, D. N. (1979). 'Laminar origins and terminations of cortical connections of the occipital lobe in the rhesus monkey', *Brain Research*, 179, 3–20.

Rodman, H. R., Gross, C. G. and Skelly, J. P. (1987). 'Adult-like properties of inferior temporal neurones in macaques, 4–6 months of age', *Society for Neuroscience Abstracts*, 13, 15–39.

Roeper, T. and Williams, E. (eds) (1987). *Parameter setting* (Dordrecht, Netherlands: Reidel).

Sackett, G. P. and Ruppenthal, G. C. (1974). 'Some factors influencing the attraction of adult female macaque monkeys to neonates', in M. Lewis, and L. Rosenblum (eds), *The Effect of the Infant on its Caregiver* (New York: Wiley).

Salzen, E. A. and Meyer, C. C. (1967). 'Imprinting: reversal of a preference established during the critical period', *Nature*, 215, 785–6.

Schanel-Klitsch E. and Siegried J. B. (1987). 'High-frequency VEP wavelets in early infancy: a preliminary study', *Infant Behavior and Development*, 10, 325–36.

Schiller, P. H. (1985). 'A model for the generation of visually guided saccadic eye movements', in D. Rose and V. G. Dobson (eds), *Models of the Visual Cortex* (New York: John Wiley).

Shepherd, G. M. (1983). *Neurobiology* (New York: OUP).

Slater, A. M., Morison, V. and Somers, M. (1988). 'Orientation discrimination and cortical function in the human newborn', *Perception*, 17, 597–602.

——, ——, Town, C. and Rose, D. (1985). 'Movement perception and identity constancy in the newborn baby', *British Journal of Developmental Psychology*, 3, 211–20.

Sluckin, W. (1972). *Imprinting and early learning* (2nd ed), (London: Methuen).

Souther, A. and Banks, M. (1979). 'The human face: A view from the infants eye', paper presented at the meeting of the Society for Research in Child Development, San Franciso, CA. (see Maurer 1985).

Spalding, D. A. (1873). 'Instinct, with original observations on young animals', *Macmillan's Magazine*, 27, 282–93.

Stampalija A. and Kostovic I. (1981). 'The laminar organisation of the superior colliculus (SC) in the human fetus', in Huber A. and Klein D. (eds), *Neurogenetics and Neuro-opthalmology* (North Holland: Elsevier).

Strauss, S. (ed.) (1982) *U-shaped Behavioural Growth* (New York: Academic Press).

Stucki, M., Kaufmann-Hayoz, R. and Kaufmann, F. (1987). 'Infants' recognition of a face revealed through motion: contribution of internal facial movement and head movement', *Journal of Experimental Child Psychology*, 44, 80–91.

Swartz, K. B. (1983). 'Species discrimination in infant Pigtail Macaques with pictorial stimuli', *Developmental Psychobiology*, 16, 219–31.

Ten Cate, C. (1984). *On the Ontogeny of Species Recognition in Zebra Finches* Ph.D. thesis, University of Groningen.

—— (1987). 'Sexual preferences in zebra finch males raised by two species: II The internal representation resulting from double imprinting', *Animal Behavior*, 35, 321–31.

—— (1989). 'Behavioral Development: towards understanding processes', in P. P. G. Bateson and P. Klopfer (eds), *Perspectives in Ethology, vol. 8* (New York: Plenum Press).

Van Essen, D. C. (1985). 'Functional organisation of primate visual cortex', in A. Peters and E. G. Jones (eds), *Cerebral Cortex, Vol. 3* (New York: Plenum).

Wu, H. M. H., Holmes, W. G., Medina, S. R. and Sackett, G. T. (1980). 'Kin preference in infant *Macaca Nemistrina*', *Nature*, 285, 225–7.

Wurtz, R. H. and Albano, J. E. (1980). 'Visual-motor function in the primate superior colliculus', *Annual Review of Neuroscience*, 3, 189–226.

Yakovlev, P. I. and Lecours, A. R. (1967). 'The myelogenetic cycles of regional maturation of the brain', In A. Minokowski (ed.), *Regional Development of the Brain in Early Life* (Philadelphia, PA: Davis).

Zajonc, R. B., Wilson, W. R. and Rajecki, D. W. (1975). 'Affiliation and social discrimination produced by brief exposure in day-old domestic chicks', *Animal Behaviour*, 23, 131–8.

Index